3 9082 01542869 4

ANSWERS
FOR
MANAGERS

Adam Radzik
Sharon Emek

Redford Township District Library
25320 West Six Mile Road
Redford, MI 48240

www.redford.lib.mi.us

Hours:

Mon–Thur 10–8:30
Fri–Sat   10–5
Sunday (School Year) 12–5

COPY 20 9A

658
R

Radzik, Adam.
    Answers for managers / Adam Radzik, Sharon
Emek. -- New York, NY : AMACOM, c1990.

    210 p.

    ISBN 0-8144-7744-5(pbk.) : $15.95

30296

    1. Management.   I. Emek, Sharon.   II.
Title.

9

90-55207
MARC

Redford Township Library
15150 Norborne
Redford, MI 48239
531-5960

This book is available at a special
discount when ordered in bulk quantities.
For information, contact Special Sales Department,
AMACOM, a division of American Management Association,
135 West 50th Street, New York, NY 10020.

This publication is designed to provide accurate and authoritative information in regard to the subject matter covered. It is sold with the understanding that the publisher is not engaged in rendering legal, accounting, or other professional service. If legal advice or other expert assistance is required, the services of a competent professional person should be sought.

Library of Congress Cataloging-in-Publication Data

Radzik, Adam.
    Answers for managers / Adam Radzik, Sharon Emek.
        p.   cm.
    Includes index.
    ISBN 0-8144-7744-5
    1. Management.   I. Emek, Sharon.   II. Title.
    HD31.R15   1990   90-55207
    658—dc20   CIP

© 1990 Adam Radzik and Sharon Emek.
All rights reserved.
Printed in the United States of America.

This publication may not be reproduced,
stored in a retrieval system,
or transmitted in whole or in part,
in any form or by any means, electronic,
mechanical, photocopying, recording, or otherwise,
without the prior written permission of AMACOM,
a division of American Management Association,
135 West 50th Street, New York, NY 10020.

Printing number

10 9 8 7 6 5 4 3 2 1

We dedicate this book to the many excellent managers with whom we have the good fortune to work, managers whose primary concern is to get their jobs done well. We salute them one and all, for managers who display vitality and commitment help keep American business strong.

CONTENTS

PREFACE

Managing people is not an easy job. Some of the problems that arise are annoying, silly, and childish. Others are quite complex, delicate, and challenging. This book is about those problems, the kinds of problems managers face on a daily basis: motivating, supervising, and communicating with subordinates and attempting to handle conflicts while simultaneously trying to get ahead in their own careers.

Motivating subordinates is not an easy job when you must deal with someone who hates his job or someone who procrastinates or someone who is hostile. It can be very frustrating to motivate others when you believe you've tried everything and nothing has worked.

Communicating with employees is difficult when you have to deal with someone who likes to yell, subordinates who don't open up, subordinates who don't tell the truth, and meetings that go nowhere.

Supervising subordinates is very challenging when you must deal with hiring, firing, training, disciplining, evaluating, delegating, and problem-solving.

Handling conflict can be trying when you have to deal with people who don't get along, or professional conflict makers, or closed minds, or subordinates you are afraid to fire for fear you will not find competent replacements.

Getting ahead is elusive when you hate office politics, when you may think you're not the smartest guy in the world, when you're not as organized as you'd like to be, or when you're wondering about leaving your current job because the company doesn't treat you right.

This book was written because clients, executives, and managers constantly ask, "Do you have these management concepts you talk about written down somewhere?" This book is a start in that direction.

This book was compiled from questions submitted by managers. They appeared in the "Down to Business" column published by *The New York Post* and written by Adam Radzik. The problems, you will discover, are very much like your problems. This book shows you that you are not alone, that many others face similar situations, and that there *are* answers that work.

We are business-turnaround consultants. This means that we take troubled companies or specific departments and make them healthier and stronger. In each company with which we've consulted, there was at least one manager who was always striving to improve and could not rest until the significant problems were solved. This manager wanted to turn around bad situations and make them into good ones. Typically, his concerns were in the areas we have focused on in this book. This manager was deeply interested in increasing motivation, improving communication, bettering supervisory skills, reducing conflict in the workplace, and getting ahead.

This book was written for those who are or who want to be this type of manager. This book is not for the manager who says, "It's been this way for the last twenty years. It'll be this way for the next twenty, too!" The manager "who knows it all already" will not be helped by this kind of book.

But for the manager who wants to grow and become even better, this book will provide him with insights, ideas, and strategies. It will make the not-so-easy job of managing easier and more doable.

If this book helps managers to even a small degree, writing it will have been well worth the effort.

Although we fully collaborated in the writing of this book, we chose to write in the first person singular to better fit the style of the book; therefore we answer questions using *I* instead of *we*. Similarly, although the pronoun *he* is generally used, this is mostly to avoid awkwardness: Managers and employees come in both sexes.

This book includes useful action tools for you and your employees, in the form of surveys, questionnaires, and checklists. Some of the subjects addressed are: Improving Employee Motivation; Effectively Disciplining Employees; Do's and Don'ts of Delegation; and Effective Performance Evaluations. Also included in this book is a Problem-Solving Index. Readers will find it useful as it directs them to several answers to similar or related problems.

ACKNOWLEDGMENTS

We thank our children, Dov and Ilana Radzik and Aleeza, Joshua, and Yael Emek, for their understanding while we wrote and rewrote this manuscript.

We also thank Joe Weiss, whose friendship and support helped us very much during the early period of this enterprise, and David M. Wildstein, without whose generosity and caring many good events would not have come to pass.

Special thanks to Adrienne Hickey, our talented editor at AMACOM, whose excellent advice and guidance added greatly to the scope and depth of this book.

Finally, we extend our gratitude to our consulting and insurance clients who over the years have significantly enriched our lives.

Chapter One

IMPROVING MOTIVATION

Introduction

A motivated worker is a pleasure to behold. He's authentic. His heart and soul are in his work. He's imaginative. He cares. This type of worker can outdo five unmotivated ones.

The question is: Why are some subordinates motivated and racing along at 100 miles per hour while others are practically asleep on the job? And why do managers sometimes have trouble motivating themselves? This chapter focuses on both issues.

Motivation is not a mysteriously elusive force that defies understanding. It is analyzable, and, once properly identified, it can be reproduced at will. This means that by understanding what motivates or demotivates a subordinate, a manager can produce a predictable result (e.g., a rise in motivation and productivity) by exhibiting a specific behavior (e.g., giving praise).

Managers often don't realize that they have this awesome power. Motivated subordinates perform superbly and reflect positively on their bosses' ability to manage and lead. This can bring impressive rewards and successive promotions to both.

As you read this Introduction, imagine that you own an automobile with a 400-horsepower engine. You can use 40 of the horses or all 400, depending on how you fine-tune the engine. The choice is yours.

"WHAT'S THE GREATEST MOTIVATOR?"

Q: I have trouble keeping my motivation level up. I have read articles and books on the subject. I have listened to tapes and attended seminars. For a short while, the advice seems to affect me, but it wears off quickly. What am I doing wrong?

A: The various motivational devices you are using have their merits, but you may be missing the most important component—the right companions.

Unfortunately, we live in a negative society, in which people frequently broadcast messages of discouragement. Your boss may say, "That's a very big job. Do you really think you can do it?" The implication may be that you can't do it.

Your peers may be questioning the soundness of your judgment when they exclaim, "What do you need it for?" Even your friends may demotivate you and feed your insecurities when they helpfully remind you that it's a cold, hard world out there.

Many people are jealous, and some do not want their world disturbed by your ambitions. In fact, many people will attempt to persuade you that you can't do whatever you have set your mind to do. Unless these people have constructive and concrete criticisms, try to interact with them as little as possible.

If you examine the lives of successful inventors, scientists, writers, and businesspeople, you will find that their biggest battle was warding off the opinions of supposedly knowledgeable colleagues and friends who continually preached abandoning the challenge. This is life's greatest demotivator. Examine the people around you and you will discover the demotivators among them.

On the other hand, life also gives us people who nurture and inspire. Seek out companions who have confidence in your ability and share your aspirations. Make it your business to be in their company as often as possible. Their positive messages will bolster your motivation and help you face the disappointments that are part of reaching any goal.

"I HATE MY JOB."

Q: I'm successful. I work for a good company, yet I'm miserable. I am unmotivated and feel tortured by my daily tasks. My lunches are getting longer, and I am looking for reasons to take business trips. I've reached the goals I set out to attain, and my peers admire and envy my success. So why am I so unhappy?

A: I'll bet that:

1. Your role in the organization has changed over the years.
2. The need for someone to handle certain complexities of the business has forced you to take on roles and exhibit skills that you didn't bargain for and don't like.
3. You find yourself saying, "I never realized my job as a manager would be like this. Had I known, I would never have taken this position."

People like you even begin to call their office The Dungeon.

What should you do? Here are four related suggestions:

1. Keep a diary for two weeks where you list each business activity in which you are involved.
2. Adjacent to each item, note whether you perform this function well in your own eyes and in the eyes of your peers.
3. Record what you like and what you dislike about this responsibility.
4. Then list the names of individuals who might be trained to take over the responsibilities you no longer wish to fulfill. Delegate only after the appropriate amount of training, support, supervision, and latitude; otherwise you may tend to say, "See, I knew I was right all along. I have to do this myself."

It is true that managers sometimes experience physical or psychological burnout, but when that is not the case, give careful consideration to these suggestions about Executive Dungeonitis. It can pose a severe threat to any career.

"MORALE IS POOR AND NO ONE CARES."

Q: As personnel director, I see that morale is low, productivity is substandard, and several of our key staff are actively looking for positions elsewhere. When I raise these issues to upper management, they tell me, "It's not *that* bad and you can't make everyone happy." How do I convince them that our problem is not small and needs to be dealt with?

A:
Your company is fortunate to have you on board. It's clear that you have your eyes and ears wide open and that you care. Unfortunately, the phenomenon that you have described is rampant in American business. The problem stems from these misconceptions:

1. The belief that only a few employees are unhappy
2. The belief that the unhappy employees are bad apples who would be unhappy under the best conditions

Your task should be to provide an objective method of ascertaining how the majority of employees really feel. An excellent tool, devised specifically for this purpose, is the employee-attitude survey. Here, employees are asked to describe anonymously how they feel about working for their company and to rate aspects such as their company's benefits or supervisory style.

I highly recommend that you have your employees complete this survey and that you use their responses to educate management on the true dimensions of employee sentiment.

Attitude surveys administered by my consulting firm have sometimes yielded surprising results. On occasion, employees are unhappy with the benefits package. Sometimes we discover that the employees don't know what their benefits package offers. In these instances, the employers were spending a sizable sum of money on benefits but, because of misinformation or lack of information, the employees were unappreciative and resentful.

Other surveys brought other surprises—a sentiment that the boss did not care about the business and was about to unload it, and a sentiment that the management viewed and treated the employees like drones. These beliefs had no foundation in truth and were later dispelled.

Use the attitude survey to demonstrate to the people you work for what companywide attitudes really are. You might wish to use the following Employee-Attitude Survey.

Action Tool: An Employee-Attitude Survey

The purpose of this survey is to determine how your employees feel about the various aspects of their jobs, the management, and the company. Use the form to gauge their overall attitude and which specific factors are affecting that attitude. Since the survey is divided into areas, it can help you determine if employees feel especially positive or negative about aspects of their jobs. Remember, it is very important that employees be as objective as possible in completing this survey.

Scoring Procedure

To determine attitude, circle the number that applies to each item, based on the following scale:

1 = very poor   3 = fair

2 = poor   4 = good

5 = excellent

	Very Poor	Poor	Fair	Good	Excellent
Compensation and Benefits					
1. The salary paid for my position is:	1	2	3	4	5
2. The health insurance benefits are:	1	2	3	4	5
3. The pension plan is:	1	2	3	4	5

Subtotal: _____

	Very Poor	Poor	Fair	Good	Excellent

4. The number of sick days I receive is: 1   2   3   4   5

5. The number of vacation days I receive is: 1   2   3   4   5

6. The number of holidays I receive is: 1   2   3   4   5

Supervisory Practices

7. The orientation I was given when I was
   hired was: 1   2   3   4   5

8. The training I received for my job was: 1   2   3   4   5

9. When the company fires someone, its
   judgment is usually: 1   2   3   4   5

10. The manner in which I have been
    evaluated is: 1   2   3   4   5

11. The manner in which my supervisor
    speaks to me is: 1   2   3   4   5

12. The openness of my superiors to
    feedback is: 1   2   3   4   5

13. The recognition I get when I do a good
    job is: 1   2   3   4   5

14. Managerial skill in resolving conflicts
    is: 1   2   3   4   5

15. The company's regard for the importance
    of my work is: 1   2   3   4   5

Subtotal: _____

	Very Poor	Poor	Fair	Good	Excellent

16. My level of understanding as to what is expected of me is: 1 2 3 4 5

17. The manner in which I am disciplined is: 1 2 3 4 5

18. The opportunity for airing grievances is: 1 2 3 4 5

19. The amount of help I can get from my supervisor is: 1 2 3 4 5

20. The probability of getting a clear answer from my supervisor is: 1 2 3 4 5

21. Overall, the response I get when I take initiative is: 1 2 3 4 5

22. The general skill level of managers is: 1 2 3 4 5

Specific Position

23. The interest level of my job is: 1 2 3 4 5

24. The level of security I feel in my job is: 1 2 3 4 5

25. The resources I have to do my job with are: 1 2 3 4 5

26. The cooperation I receive from my peers is: 1 2 3 4 5

27. My work schedule is: 1 2 3 4 5

28. My personal safety in my work environment is: 1 2 3 4 5

Subtotal: _____

	Very Poor	Poor	Fair	Good	Excellent

29. Overall, the company's treatment of me has been: 　1　2　3　4　5

30. I would describe the job I have now as: 1　2　3　4　5

Career Development

31. My career opportunities in this company are: 　1　2　3　4　5

32. From my point of view, the promotion process is: 　1　2　3　4　5

33. The possibility that I will want to be employed here five years from now is: 1　2　3　4　5

Company Facilities

34. My physical work environment is: 　1　2　3　4　5

35. The condition of the lunchroom facility is: 　1　2　3　4　5

36. The condition of the restroom is: 　1　2　3　4　5

Company Communication

37. The amount of information given to me about what's going on at the company is: 　1　2　3　4　5

Company Image

38. The manner in which the company keeps promises is: 　1　2　3　4　5

Subtotal: _____

	Very Poor	Poor	Fair	Good	Excellent
39. In terms of not playing favorites, the company is:	1	2	3	4	5
40. The company's ability to make decisions is:	1	2	3	4	5
41. The level of caring that exists for the individual employee is:	1	2	3	4	5
42. The fairness of the company's layoff policy is:	1	2	3	4	5
43. The company's adherence to the law is:	1	2	3	4	5
44. The company's adherence to a code of ethics is:	1	2	3	4	5
45. The general morale level in the company is:	1	2	3	4	5
46. The chances of my recommending a friend to work here are:	1	2	3	4	5
47. The chances of this company existing ten years from now are:	1	2	3	4	5
48. Overall, when I describe this company to others, I say it is:	1	2	3	4	5

Company Structure

	Very Poor	Poor	Fair	Good	Excellent
49. The internal organization of the company is:	1	2	3	4	5
50. As a first step, I think this attitude survey is:	1	2	3	4	5

Total: _____

Scoring Guide

Add up the scores for each factor and divide by 50 to get employee attitude.

Interpretation Key

Check your score against the following scale:

1.0–1.5 = very poor—immediate attention required

1.6–2.5 = poor—make this a priority

2.6–3.5 = fair—okay but needs improvement

3.6–4.5 = good—you're on the right track

4.6–5.0 = excellent—you're doing a great job

"I NEED TO INCREASE PRODUCTIVITY."

Q: Our costs are too high and we are losing orders to our competition. As a result, I'm under pressure to increase employee productivity and performance. I have about fifteen employees. Can you give me some ideas?

A:

I do have an idea for you. It's not original, but it does increase productivity. It's saying thank you to employees.

Think about it. When is the last time you thanked or complimented your employees for something special they did or for just doing their jobs well day in and day out? It's human nature to like praise and appreciation, and people are motivated to work for them.

I often ask my clients, "Do you want to make a thousand dollars in the next five minutes? Go give an employee a word of praise. His work rate will increase, his motivation level will rise, and he will pass along his mood to others."

Don't give false compliments, because that will backfire, but search for something that is legitimately worth praising. Chances are that the praised employee will tell his co-workers, his wife, his mother, his friends, and the guys in the bowling league.

There seems to be no scarcity of negative feedback in our society. Indeed, we are quick to criticize but slow to compliment. We tend to make a big deal about a mistake and to take good work for granted. "That's what they get paid for," managers tell me.

Another aberrant philosophy runs like this: If you give them a raise, first thing you know they'll want another raise, a promotion, an office with a window and a view, and all kinds of special privileges. To keep them in line, you've got to keep them thinking that you're not happy with their performance.

We would all do well to remember the saying, "It's much better to have one man work with you than to have ten men work for you." A word of appreciation can help you develop the kind of people who will work with you to make your company a powerful force in the marketplace.

Seeing that employees get the proper training, take part in goal setting, and/or have specific objectives built into their performance-appraisal system can have far-reaching impact on the issue of productivity as well. See Chapter Three, "No one is happy with evaluations" and "We don't achieve our goals."

"HOW DO I KEEP ENTHUSIASM HIGH?"

Q: I've put together a team of employees to work on a special project. I want to be certain that these people see this project through and that their level of motivation stays high. How do I accomplish this?

A:

You need to get to know each individual employee really well. Your purpose in this is to establish a motivational profile to learn what motive or collection of motives affects each one. Is it achievement? Is it public recognition? Is it monetary compensation? Is it a secure position? Is it being first?

Often, the approach to employee motivation is too simplistic. Human beings are not all the same. They come in a vast assortment of sizes, shapes, and colors. The same is true of their motivational profiles. To one man, chairing the committee is important. To another, saving time is paramount. To a third, freedom from worry is the ultimate objective.

Your goal should be to find out what each person is looking for and to ensure that his needs, as much as possible, are continually met. If you are able to accomplish this task, your employees will remain dedicated to your project, and their performance level will be superb. In this respect, human behavior is predictable.

A classic misapplication of motivation technique occurred with an executive who ran a personnel placement agency. He offered his manager a brand-new $40,000 Jaguar if she could achieve a certain sales goal. He was very proud of his generosity and cleverness. Upon speaking with this woman, I discovered that she was not only *not* motivated by this offer but she was annoyed. "What will I do with it?" she asked. "I can't afford the gas; I can't afford the repairs. The way I handle cars it'll spend half the time in the shop, and it's also too ostentatious. I'm a simple woman and I'm the sole support of two sons. What I need is money, not a Jaguar. The only reason he offered me that car was because that's what *he* would want. He doesn't care about what *I* want or need!" The executive's attempt at motivation had backfired.

In a different situation, an executive read his employee correctly. He knew that money was not the answer for this employee. Instead, he offered a promotion and the opportunity for more input. The strategy worked and the employee responded beautifully to the promise of a reward for which he had yearned.

The point is that managers need to use the right motivational tool to achieve the desired result.

To assist you in discovering your employees' motivational profiles, you might wish to use the following Employee-Motivation Profile.

Action Tool: Employee-Motivation Profile

There is no such thing as a lazy person, only an unmotivated person. *Lazy* is only a label we give a person who is not interested in doing something. But if someone offered a lazy person $100 or a promotion to move his chair from one side of the room to another, most likely that person would do it. The key to getting people to do things is to motivate them, and to do this we must know what would motivate them since not all people are motivated by the same things.

The purpose of this survey is for the manager to identify individual employee motivations. Have your employees fill out the survey, and then use it to focus on what motivates individuals to do their best. Once the motivational factors are identified, you can devise methods to better motivate specific individuals.

Scoring Procedure

To determine motivational factors, circle the number that applies to each item using the following scale:

1 = marginally important to me

2 = important to me

3 = very important to me

Categories that have no importance should be left blank.

The areas below represent the drives or motivations that are important to me in my work:

	Marginally Important	Important	Very Important
1. Receiving praise from my superiors	1	2	3
2. Receiving praise from my co-workers	1	2	3
3. Receiving praise from my subordinates	1	2	3
4. Receiving respect from my superiors	1	2	3
5. Receiving respect from my co-workers	1	2	3
6. Receiving respect from my subordinates	1	2	3
7. Having a sense of achievement	1	2	3
8. Advancing my career	1	2	3
9. Receiving monetary compensation	1	2	3
10. Receiving company benefits (health insurance, pension)	1	2	3
11. Being secure in my senior years	1	2	3
12. Doing interesting work	1	2	3
13. Having learning opportunities	1	2	3
14. Having opportunity for input	1	2	3
15. Being cared for as a human being	1	2	3
16. Enjoying my daily duties	1	2	3
17. Having the opportunity to be creative	1	2	3
18. Being efficient	1	2	3
19. Being confident	1	2	3
20. Being knowledgeable	1	2	3
21. Exerting influence over others	1	2	3
22. Being part of a prestigious company	1	2	3

"HE CAN'T GET THINGS DONE."

Q: I have a talented employee who is a procrastinator and lazy. I've told him so many times. I've given him books to read and sent him to seminars. Nothing seems to help. I don't know what to do.

A: You need to fully understand the problem. Why do people procrastinate? They procrastinate not because of some terrible flaw in their personality but because they fear or dislike some aspect of the activity assigned them.

The remedy for this behavior is to identify the problem and solve it.

A president of a family-owned company was always procrastinating when it came to making decisions. He did this because he didn't have the information he needed and was afraid of making the wrong decision. When he learned how to get more information, he stopped procrastinating.

A director procrastinated in submitting his monthly report. His problem was that he was unsure of his writing ability. A brief writing course solved his problem.

A sales manager procrastinated in firing a salesperson. He felt guilty because he had brought the person into the company. Eventually, when he realized that everyone, including the salesperson, is responsible for his own fate, the sales manager was able to proceed with the dismissal.

You say that your employee is lazy, but I really don't believe that the quality of laziness exists. When people are not motivated to do a particular task, we punish them by calling them lazy. But if you offered a lazy person his favorite activity, you'd see how fast he'd move.

The real problem is that either the motivations attached to the job don't attract this "lazy" person or the rewards offered are not high enough.

Also, personality labels that people use as pressure can be too effective. The person you're labeling becomes convinced you're right, and the behavior you wished to erase becomes even more entrenched.

Beware of calling employees names. After a while, they may believe you and begin to act the part. A better tactic would be to discover the cause of the procrastination and resolve it.

"MY EMPLOYEES LOOK UNFRIENDLY."

Q: As a manager, I walk around to see how everybody is doing. Do you know what I see most? Sour faces. My employees look angry and unfriendly. Our shipments are late and the machines are not well-attended. What should I do?

A: If many of your employees are unhappy, something in their work environment is causing them to feel that way. Don't assume their gripes are all monetary. Nor should you assume that they are malcontents who complain no matter what. These interpretations of employee behavior are just plain silly.

If your employees are unhappy, look for the reason for their unhappiness. Don't try to change their attitude without trying to solve their functional work problems. Once the reasons are addressed and corrected, the attitude will improve by itself.

For example, a shipping manager was unhappy because he couldn't get the daily decisions he needed in order to do his job. Understandably, his attitude was poor. A data processing manager was unhappy because people were not cooperating with him. His expressions reflected his discontent.

My point? Nobody comes to work and says, "Okay, today is Tuesday. This would be a good day to act hostile and angry. Also, I think I'll break a machine after lunch." If your employees are unhappy, there are reasons and usually pretty good ones.

Forthright questions, asked in private and with assurances that there will be no repercussion, sometimes elicit honest discussions of problems. Other revealing methods include a suggestion box placed in a public place and quality circle groups with rotating representation. Consultation with human resource personnel, managers of other departments, or communications consultants will also prove fruitful.

Remember, employees are just like you and me. They'd much rather be happy than unhappy.

"I'VE TRIED EVERYTHING."

Q: No one can say that I haven't tried hard to keep my subordinates motivated. They receive good salaries, a handsome benefits package, and a nice-looking work environment. In spite of all this, their work shows that they don't care. They are constantly looking at the clock and can't wait to leave. I am coming to the conclusion that it doesn't pay to be nice to people. Maybe if I fired a few of them, I'd get better results. What do you think?

A: It appears that you've been doing the right things but maybe not enough of them. If I were you, I would take a hard look at some of the following areas as well:

- Do you allow your subordinates to participate in decision making or do you simply expect them to carry out your directives?
- Do your subordinates have expectations in terms of promotions and opportunities for increased responsibilities? Do some believe you've made promises that have not been fulfilled?
- Do you reward your employees in any way when they do show initiative or turn in superior performance?
- Do the influential persons in your organization, whether they are managers or employees, broadcast positive or negative messages?
- Do your employees get along well with you or is there an undercurrent of hostility, resentment, and lack of mutual respect?

With motivation, it's important to remember that *people will work for money, but except under extreme privation, they resist working for money alone.* They also want recognition, security, and opportunity, just to name a few other incentives.

To determine your subordinates' motivational profiles and how to chart their improvement, you might want to use the following survey, Improving Employee Motivation: Twenty Important Factors.

Action Tool: Improving Employee Motivation: Twenty Important Factors

One of the keys to a profitable business is motivated employees. Motivated employees are more productive, more willing to share ideas, more willing to help co-workers and the company, more loyal, and so on.

Many times, our perceptions of the level of employee motivation (companywide) and which factors affect that level are different from the perceptions of our employees.

This rating tool identifies the most common factors that affect employee motivation and helps you find the level of employee motivation at your company and which factors are affecting that level.

Use this survey on yourself. Answer the questions as you believe your employees would. It's very important to be as objective as possible when completing this survey.

You should also have this survey completed by your employees, anonymously rating you in this area so that you can compare your perceptions to those of your employees.

Scoring Procedure

To determine the employees' overall motivational level, circle the number that applies, based on the following scale:

1 = never   3 = half of the time

2 = sometimes 4 = most of the time

5 = always

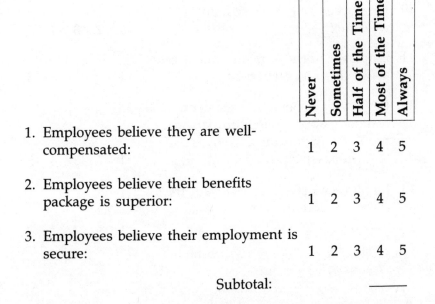

	Never	Sometimes	Half of the Time	Most of the Time	Always
1. Employees believe they are well-compensated:	1	2	3	4	5
2. Employees believe their benefits package is superior:	1	2	3	4	5
3. Employees believe their employment is secure:	1	2	3	4	5

Subtotal: _____

	Never	Sometimes	Half of the Time	Most of the Time	Always
4. Employees believe the company promotes from within, where it is possible:	1	2	3	4	5
5. Employees believe their achievements are recognized:	1	2	3	4	5
6. Employees believe there are good possibilities for career advancement:	1	2	3	4	5
7. Employees believe they are fairly evaluated:	1	2	3	4	5
8. Employees believe they are fairly disciplined:	1	2	3	4	5
9. Employees believe their contributions are valued:	1	2	3	4	5
10. Employees believe their input is welcome:	1	2	3	4	5
11. Employees believe management cares about them as human beings:	1	2	3	4	5
12. Employees believe management responds appropriately to personal problems within the employee's life (e.g., illness):	1	2	3	4	5
13. Employees believe working for the company adds to their personal prestige:	1	2	3	4	5

Subtotal: _____

	Never	Sometimes	Half of the Time	Most of the Time	Always

14. Employees believe they can influence the opinions of their supervisors: 1   2   3   4   5

15. Employees believe the company is well-organized: 1   2   3   4   5

16. Employees believe management's judgment is good: 1   2   3   4   5

17. Employees believe the company is progressive in its field: 1   2   3   4   5

18. Employees believe the company will treat them well during their senior years: 1   2   3   4   5

19. Employees believe that when the company dismisses employees, it is justified: 1   2   3   4   5

20. Employees believe they are treated fairly and the company does not indulge in favoritism or prejudice: 1   2   3   4   5

Total: _____

Scoring Guide

Add up the scores for each factor and divide by 20 to get the level of employee motivation.

Interpretation Key

Check your score against the following scale:

1.0–1.5 = motivation level dangerously low

1.6–2.5 = poor motivation level

2.6–3.5 = average motivation level

3.6–4.5 = good motivation level

4.6–5.0 = very high motivation level

Chapter Two

IMPROVING
COMMUNICATION

Introduction

One of the marvelous qualities of each human being is that he
carries around in his head a tremendous computer that re-
cords all the knowledge and experience of his life, a giant
computer bank of inestimable value. Communication allows
the computer banks of two people to interface and benefit
from each other's accumulated data and wisdom. What a
resource! What an opportunity!

Communication is nothing more than a pickup and delivery service. It picks up from you and delivers to someone else.
Sometimes, however, this sharing does not take place. The
communication process goes awry. This problem happens
when what you intended to send is received in a totally
different form. As a psychologist friend of mine says, "He
sent a warm fuzzy, and what she received was a cold prickly."

This chapter discusses this problem. Our minds are not
perfect instruments. We sometimes send the wrong message,
and we sometimes misperceive what was sent to us. It also
happens that we say one thing and mean another, or that we
don't think enough before we speak. Sometimes we take a
stray and careless thought and present that as our opinion

31

when that thought does not represent our true position. This chapter reflects Emerson's adage, "It's a luxury to be understood."

Some of the subjects of interest to the reader include discerning if employees tell the truth, understanding employee reactions, and being close with employees.

"SHE SOUNDS LIKE A DRILL SERGEANT."

Q: Our telephone receptionist does about twenty different things during her workday. She takes care of travel arrangements, orders lunch, and straightens up the office, but she's very high-strung. When she answers the phone, she sounds like a marine drill sergeant barking at the troops. We've talked to her about this several times, but it doesn't seem to do any good. What do you suggest I do?

A: First of all, you should put this woman in charge of all travel arrangements, lunch orders, and office clean-ups. Apparently, she does these tasks very well. But as strange as this sounds, this woman's job assignment is not my greatest concern.

Most importantly and as soon as possible, you should get yourself someone else to answer your phone. Why? Because a pleasant receptionist will attract your customers and an irritated receptionist will drive them away. Almost like magnets, people are drawn by a positive personality and are repelled by a negative one. This can have a big dollar impact on your business.

I know of one stock brokerage company that pays its receptionist in excess of $40,000 a year. When she answers the phone, she sounds delighted that you're calling. You can definitely "hear" her smile as she speaks. You begin to feel as if your call made her day. Unwittingly, you begin looking for reasons to call and hear that welcoming voice.

The attitude of the receptionist can set the tone for the conversation that follows. Does she sound annoyed? Does she keep you on hold without explanation? Does she respond to questions with "I don't know anything about that; I just answer the phone"?

If you are wondering about the telephone manners of your receptionist or of other people within your organization, have someone call your office. You may be surprised at what he reports hearing. If possible, and if there are no legal restrictions, tape-record the conversation. As is often the case in business, the surprises are usually unhappy ones.

"HE DOESN'T COMMUNICATE EFFECTIVELY."

Q: One employee who reports to me is a supervisor. His car is the first one in the parking lot in the morning and the last one out at night. His staff thinks he's okay, but they say he doesn't communicate correctly. When I ask them to be more specific, they can't put their objections into words. This supervisor doesn't have a speech impediment. What problem can he have with the way he talks?

A: Communicating correctly is a skill like any other. It can be learned, and frankly, it should be taught. Unfortunately, our schools often fill the young with esoteric trivia they may never use and neglect to give them basic courses in communication.

Help the supervisor who reports to you become aware of his strengths and weaknesses. Capitalize on his good qualities and give him the help he needs to overcome his weak ones, either through your own expertise or by bringing in an outside professional. If the supervisor is worthwhile, don't hesitate to spend money in this regard.

To help you identify your subordinate's communication profile, you might wish to use the following survey, Do's and Don'ts of Communication.

Action Tool: Do's and Don'ts of Communication

How a person communicates with others affects motivation and productivity on the job. Being a good communicator is vital for managers and employees. The following survey will assist you in identifying those areas that need improvement.

Use this survey on yourself. Answer the questions as you believe your employees would answer them. Remember, it's important to be as objective as possible when completing this survey.

You should also have this survey completed by your employees, anonymously rating you in this area so that you can compare your perceptions with those of your employees.

Scoring Procedure

To determine your overall communication level, circle the number that applies to each item, based on the following scale:

1 = never   3 = half of the time

2 = sometimes 4 = most of the time

5 = always

	Never	Sometimes	Half of the Time	Most of the Time	Always
1. Takes into account the intrinsic interest of the audience in the subject	1	2	3	4	5
2. Takes into account the attention span of the audience	1	2	3	4	5
3. Maintains good eye contact	1	2	3	4	5
4. Maintains good body posture	1	2	3	4	5
5. Gives only the necessary details	1	2	3	4	5
6. Speaks at the right speed and volume	1	2	3	4	5
7. Speaks distinctly	1	2	3	4	5
8. Allows the other person to participate	1	2	3	4	5
9. Displays signs of listening (e.g., nodding, smiling, commenting)	1	2	3	4	5
10. Allows the other person to complete his thoughts without interruption	1	2	3	4	5
11. Emotions are appropriate to the content of the thoughts expressed	1	2	3	4	5
12. Stays on the subject and does not ramble	1	2	3	4	5
13. Facial expressions attract the listener	1	2	3	4	5
14. Possesses and uses a rich vocabulary to express ideas	1	2	3	4	5

Subtotal: _____

	Never	Sometimes	Half of the Time	Most of the Time	Always
15. Uses humor where appropriate	1	2	3	4	5
16. Expresses ideas effectively but does not repeat himself	1	2	3	4	5
17. Uses words that the audience understands	1	2	3	4	5
18. Presents ideas in their proper perspective	1	2	3	4	5
19. Exudes a confident, in-control manner	1	2	3	4	5
20. Knows when to stop talking	1	2	3	4	5

Total: _____

Scoring Guide

Add up the scores for each factor and divide by 20 to determine overall communication level.

Interpretation Key

Check your score against the following scale:

1.0–1.5 = very poor communicator

1.6–2.5 = poor communicator

2.6–3.5 = average communicator

3.6–4.5 = good communicator

4.6–5.0 = excellent communicator

"IF I YELL,
SO WHAT?"

Q: I was recently called into the president's office and criticized for the way I discipline my employees. Apparently, there are complaints that I yell and scream. They are also saying that I am insulting. The president told me he wants me to tone down and find a better way. This is easy for him to say. He doesn't have to deal with them. They don't listen unless I rant and rave. What should I do?

A:
The word *discipline* implies teaching and learning. One of its specific definitions is "training intended to produce a specified character or pattern of behavior."

You are not teaching; you are browbeating. Your employees are not learning. They continue to exhibit the behaviors that you find unacceptable. Furthermore, your own career will suffer.

It sounds as if the president of your company believes, as many people do, that the louder you raise your voice, the greater the likelihood that you are wrong and the other person is right.

When you begin to yell at people, they become emotionally involved with your yelling. They stop hearing your message and focus instead on their embarrassment and loss of dignity.

Think about your own personality. If I wanted you to change the way you were doing something, do you believe the best technique for me to use would be to take you to my office, or better yet, to a crowded public place, and start screaming at you and insulting you? Would that get you moving in the right direction?

Reasonable employees should be dealt with reasonably, no yelling, no insults. Unreasonable employees should not be dealt with at all; they should be fired, because yelling and insults will not help anyway.

To determine what your approach to discipline is and what your strengths and weaknesses are, you might wish to use the following survey, Effectively Disciplining Employees.

Action Tool: Effectively Disciplining Employees

Disciplining employees properly has great impact on attitude, motivation, and productivity of employees. If clear behavior and performance guidelines are not established or if the discipline is too harsh, lenient, or unfair, employees will not act as a cooperative work force and will not put in the extra effort required to complete their work quickly, effectively, and profitably.

Use this survey to determine how effectively you discipline your employees. Rate yourself by answering the questions as you believe your employees would answer them. Remember, it's very important to be as objective as possible when completing the survey.

You should also have this survey completed by your employees, anonymously rating you in this area so that you can compare your perceptions with those of your employees.

Scoring Procedure

To determine how well you discipline, circle the number that applies to each item, based on the following scale:

$$1 = \text{never} \qquad 3 = \text{half of the time}$$

$$2 = \text{sometimes} \quad 4 = \text{most of the time}$$

$$5 = \text{always}$$

	Never	Sometimes	Half of the Time	Most of the Time	Always
1. Clearly explains established company rules and guidelines	1	2	3	4	5
2. Makes job expectations clear	1	2	3	4	5
3. Establishes clear performance standards from the outset	1	2	3	4	5
4. Makes certain that employees have a clear understanding of the consequences for inappropriate behavior	1	2	3	4	5

Subtotal: _____

	Never	Sometimes	Half of the Time	Most of the Time	Always
5. Gives employees frequent feedback on work behaviors	1	2	3	4	5
6. Explains to employees that salary increases depend on work behaviors	1	2	3	4	5
7. Takes action when an employee breaks a rule	1	2	3	4	5
8. Does not act in anger	1	2	3	4	5
9. Treats each case individually	1	2	3	4	5
10. Informs the employee of the charges against him	1	2	3	4	5
11. Does not assume the offender is guilty before obtaining all of the evidence	1	2	3	4	5
12. Gives the employee an impartial review of the action	1	2	3	4	5
13. Gives the employee an opportunity to reply to the charges	1	2	3	4	5
14. Is considerate of the offender's feelings	1	2	3	4	5
15. Is consistent in dealing with employees	1	2	3	4	5
16. Is not overly harsh in dealing with employees	1	2	3	4	5

Subtotal: _____

	Never	Sometimes	Half of the Time	Most of the Time	Always
17. Is not overly permissive in dealing with employees	1	2	3	4	5
18. Criticizes the offender in private as opposed to in public	1	2	3	4	5
19. Assists the employee in finding ways to change the inappropriate behavior	1	2	3	4	5
20. Keeps careful records of each significant infraction	1	2	3	4	5

Total: _____

Scoring Guide

Add up the scores for each factor and divide by 20 to determine how well you discipline employees.

Interpretation Key

Check your score against the following scale:

1.0–1.5 = very poor disciplinarian
1.6–2.5 = poor disciplinarian
2.6–3.5 = fair disciplinarian
3.6–4.5 = good disciplinarian
4.6–5.0 = excellent disciplinarian

"MY EMPLOYEES DON'T OPEN UP."

 I don't find out about problems in my department until it's too late to solve them. I find that my employees don't open up to me and avoid contact with me as much as possible. I'm a very open guy, and I don't understand why these things are happening.

A: Many managers perceive themselves to be open with employees. They view themselves as being tolerant, broad-minded, and receptive to divergent points of view. What sometimes happens in managers' interactions with employees is the following: An employee comes in to make a suggestion. The manager is skeptical and shows it in the expression on his face and in the tone of his voice. When the employee continues to present his viewpoint, the manager begins to get annoyed, even angry, and cuts the conversation short.

The manager is unaware of the true nature of his response. He views himself as being firm when in truth he is acting negatively and almost hostile.

Faced with this kind of reaction, the employee walks out of the office thinking to himself, "What an idiot I was for going in there to talk to him. This is the last time I'll do that."

If you want to encourage honest employee communication, learn to disagree while still maintaining a pleasant expression and tone. (If need be, have someone sit in and observe to make certain the quality of the interaction is positive.)

Additional reasons that stymie employee communication are: the perception that the manager is always busy and becomes annoyed if disturbed, the perception that the manager gives lip service to the ideas suggested by employees but never implements them, and the perception that the manager thinks employee problems are simply unimportant.

Managers would do well to work on improving their listening skills, observing the nonverbal communications of their employees, and asking employees frequently for their opinion on a wide variety of issues.

"ARE THEY TELLING ME THE TRUTH?"

 The supervisors who work under me have foremen below them. We have meetings for them to report to me about what is going on in the plant, but frankly, I am not sure if they always tell me the truth or if they simply tell me what they think I want to hear. What do you advise?

A: The natural tendency among human beings is to make themselves look good to their supervisor (the CYA or Cover Your — — — method). Typically, people do not admit their mistakes. They blame them on someone in their department, reporting that "John never handed in his report." John, who was never told to hand in a report, has no idea why three months later he is informed by someone in personnel that because of a *clash of personalities* with his supervisor, he is being let go.

Your fear that you're not hearing the full truth is well-founded. People protect themselves from upper management in many ways, for example, by changing inventory levels and manufacturing reports to make them look good and by reporting that employee morale is just fine. Information tends to be censored, edited, altered, and reinterpreted.

I tell my clients to use the respect-suspect philosophy: Respect your supervisors but check up on them occasionally as well.

You should also take frequent walking tours in the plant, talk with the employees, encourage them to share their ideas and concerns with you, and at least periodically dine with them. Talk with representatives of every department several times during the year. Your employees will appreciate this, and you will get a fresh, unfiltered perspective.

"I WANT FEEDBACK."

 I'm a manager in a Fortune 500 company, and, of course, I evaluate my employees. But I am seriously interested in my own improvement. God knows, I'm not perfect. What I would like is the opportunity for my employees to evaluate me. Do any companies have such a procedure and how can it be done?

A: Yes, but very few. This is a shame because a manager can learn a great deal about himself from his subordinates.

The reason this is not a more common practice is that many managers believe being evaluated by their employees would show disrespect for their position. The rating would be a "silly report card given by a vengeful employee," they think.

Not true. This activity is not silly; it's enlightening. It's not a report card, but feedback, seldom given with vengeance. Most employees rate their managers fairly and with heart. Often they rate them too kindly.

I remember when I was teaching at a university and my students rated me. I waited with bated breath, then was warmed by their praises.

When employees do rate their managers, they should do so anonymously. Their responses should be summarized by a trusted member of the employee group and given only to the manager being rated. (Unless there are numerous complaints about the manager, there is no need to share the results with his supervisors.) Areas that should be rated include the manager's organization of his work activities and time management, as well as his motivational and human relations abilities.

If you pursue your idea of having your employees rate you, I guarantee you some fascinating reading! You will learn things about your managerial style that you never knew. Chances are you will be complimented in some ways and chided in others.

You may wish to use the following survey, Rating the Manager.

Action Tool: Rating the Manager

The purpose of this survey is to increase the communication between managers and their subordinates. Employees periodically receive feedback on their performance, but managers rarely receive feedback on their performance from subordinates. Managers can greatly benefit from such an interaction. They find it very enlightening to know how their employees view them.

First use this survey on yourself, answering the questions as you believe your employees would answer them. Remember, it's very important to be as objective as possible when completing the survey.

Then you should have this survey completed by your employees, anonymously rating you in this area so that you can compare your perceptions with those of your employees.

Scoring Procedure

To determine your score, rate each factor based on the following scale:

1 = never   3 = half of the time

2 = sometimes   4 = most of the time

5 = always

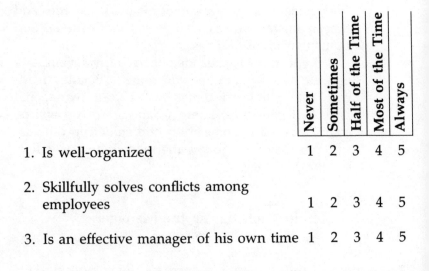

	Never	Sometimes	Half of the Time	Most of the Time	Always
1. Is well-organized	1	2	3	4	5
2. Skillfully solves conflicts among employees	1	2	3	4	5
3. Is an effective manager of his own time	1	2	3	4	5

Subtotal: _____

	Never	Sometimes	Half of the Time	Most of the Time	Always
4. Assesses employees accurately and fairly	1	2	3	4	5
5. Does not overload employees with too many projects at one time	1	2	3	4	5
6. Supplies employees with appropriate training	1	2	3	4	5
7. Motivates people to want to do their best	1	2	3	4	5
8. Does not blame employees for his own errors	1	2	3	4	5
9. Is willing to explain the work to others	1	2	3	4	5
10. Is skilled in explaining work to others	1	2	3	4	5
11. Assigns employees tasks that suit their abilities	1	2	3	4	5
12. Gives employees clear job descriptions	1	2	3	4	5
13. Does not give directives without explaining the rationale behind them	1	2	3	4	5
14. Is generous in praise of others when appropriate	1	2	3	4	5
15. Does not overplay the boss role	1	2	3	4	5

Subtotal: _____

	Never	Sometimes	Half of the Time	Most of the Time	Always
16. Is prone to recognize and reward unusual employee achievement	1	2	3	4	5
17. Responds to employee concerns about the company	1	2	3	4	5
18. Values employees' opinions	1	2	3	4	5
19. Is willing to accept employees who are not "yes" people	1	2	3	4	5
20. Understands the unavoidable human-error factor	1	2	3	4	5

Total: _____

Scoring Guide

Add up the scores for each factor and divide by 20 to determine overall evaluation.

Interpretation Key

Check your score against the following scale:

1.0–1.5 = very poor manager

1.6–2.5 = poor manager

2.6–3.5 = average manager

3.6–4.5 = good manager

4.6–5.0 = excellent manager

"HE MUST BE
ANGRY WITH ME!"

Q: I was amazed when two employees who work for me told another manager that I don't like them and am always angry at them. If anything, I favor them. They are both top performers, and I can never remember being dissatisfied with them in any way. What's happening?

A: I call this the Management Face Syndrome. It works like this:

The manager is concerned about a problem. He's full of worry and anxiety. Frank, an employee, passes him in the corridor and greets him with a smiling "Hi!" The manager, still engrossed in his situation, looks up briefly and mumbles a reply. Frank's cheerful mood plummets. "Why is he angry at me? What did I do? Maybe he doesn't think I'm doing a good job anymore because of what I said at the meeting last week."

The next day, the manager's crisis takes a turn for the worse. Frank tries greeting him again, but this time the manager doesn't even respond. Frank's worst fears have been confirmed. Unknown to the manager, his relationship with Frank is rapidly deteriorating.

Why does this happen? Employees are constantly gauging their job security and their employer's satisfaction with their performance by the expression they see on their manager's face. They assume, sometimes erroneously, that the manager's mood must be related to how he feels about them and their performance.

Managers would do well to be aware of how closely employees study and analyze their facial expressions. I know because, in the past, as an employee, I fell victim to this syndrome a few times — if about a hundred times can be considered a few.

Three effective ways to counteract the Management Face Syndrome are to:

1. Give employees frequent verbal feedback on how they are doing. This will reduce their need to speculate about your perception of them.
2. Tell employees when issues are weighing heavily on your mind and explain that your look of concern is unrelated to them.

3. When appropriate, share the troublesome issue with employees. In addition to allaying their fears, your frankness will make it possible for subordinates to assist in devising solutions or strategies that may not be readily apparent to you.

"MY BOSS DOESN'T SAY HELLO."

 I am a middle-level manager, and I work in a large company. Every morning I say hello to my employees. The president of the company is just the opposite. He never bothers to say good morning to anyone. Even if employees meet him head-on in the hall, the most they get out of him is a nod and a grunt. He does this with everybody. Why does he act this way?

A: Some bosses and managers, consciously or subconsciously, regard their subordinates as subhuman and therefore do not accord them the most basic courtesies. Others are so absorbed in their own thoughts that they literally do not see others. Some consider themselves too busy to take the time for civility. And a few are so shy that they wait for someone else to make the first move.

But whatever the reason, the behavior of unfriendly bosses has the effect of alienating their employees, and alienated employees do not put out 100 percent of their efforts. In fact, they give as little as possible.

Unfortunately, some bosses forget that employees today are not the grateful immigrants of yesteryear who were appreciative of any opportunity to feed their families. Today, employees want to be treated with respect and consideration. If their expectation is not met, they either become marginal performers or seek other employment.

The intelligent boss realizes that his company's success depends in great part upon the people who work for him. He wants them to be motivated, to keep their spirits high. He knows that their morale very directly affects his company's profits. He or his secretary remembers birthdays, anniversaries of employment, and whose son is graduating from college. This type of boss has employees who say, "We would do anything for him," or "He's such a gentleman." In his company, you can feel the respect for the employer and see the results.

When this type of boss goes into the hospital, his room looks like a florist's shop. The other type of boss also gets flowers—sent by his secretary and charged to the company, of course.

If your boss is approachable, raise the issue of his style in a delicate fashion. If he becomes furious at your *insolence*, go find yourself another boss, one with manners. Motivating employees in that type of environment is like trying to push back a tidal wave.

"I CAN'T BELIEVE HER REACTION."

 I just don't understand my employees. I had to discipline an employee for coming in late, explaining to her how her actions affected morale and how important it was for her to set an example. This is all I said to her. A few days later I found out from the bookkeeper that she now believes that I regard her overall performance as being lousy and that I would be happy if she left the company. Where does this craziness come from?

A: This problem stems from your employee's insecurity and lack of perspective, but it is in no way limited to this one employee. The tendency to inflate negative comments is a very common response that managers need to deal with.

Unfortunately, our culture is such that we focus our attention primarily on the negative and almost tangentially on the positive. (Newspaper headlines are prime examples.) The child who is chastised for failing to do homework one night can't help but notice that the nights when homework is done pass without comment. Our antennae for receiving negatives are very well-developed, but positive reception is often weak. The difference is great, a thirty-foot rooftop satellite dish versus a bent rabbit ear. We appear to have a tendency to pick up every negative signal, sometimes even the nonexistent ones, and miss the positive signals altogether.

The pattern is as you describe it. The manager points out a specific area of poor performance to the employee and the employee walks away thinking, "He thinks I'm worthless. He's probably going to fire me." The manager is now faced with a bigger problem, a totally demoralized employee.

How do you deal with this? When you call in an employee to give negative criticism, first inform him as to how you feel about the total performance record, positive and negative. Then define the issue you will be discussing. Toward the end of the session, once again review with your employee the overall evaluation of his performance. These steps will help the employee put your comments in the proper perspective and focus on the real issues, thus diminishing the imagined ones.

"NOBODY PARTICIPATES AT MEETINGS."

 The president of our company usually copies your columns and sends them to the various divisions. He suggested that I ask you about the problem I am having with my employee meetings. It's very simple: No one participates. I raise an issue and everybody stares around the room. After a while, the silence becomes embarrassing. Why is this happening?

A: Employees will not speak up at meetings if they are afraid. Some managers encourage their employees to voice their opinions, but when they do the manager responds with gritted teeth and malevolent eyes. Other managers become defensive and transform discussions into heated debates. These behaviors cause workers to clam up.

Sometimes managers think they are having a discussion, but their words and demeanor indicate a lecture. Or they perceive themselves as asking questions, but in actuality they have transformed the meeting into giving directives about company policy.

Sometimes employees cannot respond to queries because they have been caught unprepared and have to give the subject more thought before they can comment.

Occasionally, employees don't understand what is being asked of them, or do not wish to answer for fear of conflict with another employee at the meeting.

And still other employees don't speak up because they feel, "What's the use? The managers don't listen to what we have to say anyway. We don't say anything because we'd be wasting our breath."

To improve the character and tone of your meetings, be certain that the above problems are not occurring. You may also want to tell the attendees at the beginning of the meeting that later you will be asking for their opinions, and that they should be formulating their thoughts.

"OUR MEETINGS DRAG ON FOREVER."

 Although I know I need to have management meetings so that information is shared and decisions are made, my meetings rarely happen that way. They start late, we hardly ever accomplish anything, and they drag on forever. It's not that we don't have important things to discuss; we do. Why is this happening?

A:

Researchers tell us that the average manager spends 30 to 40 percent of his time in meetings. Too much of this meeting time is wasted. Here are reliable ways to resolve some of the problems:

1. Reduce the size of your meetings. The more people you invite, the more time it takes for everyone to be heard. If you want someone not present to be kept informed, send him the minutes.

2. Don't let your meetings become "tell them off" sessions in which participants are attacked. If criticism needs to be given to some employees, do so in private and don't involve the entire group.

3. Don't let your meetings be dominated by excessively talkative types who don't let others get a word in edgewise. Make sure everyone has a chance to speak.

4. Agree upon a reasonable time for each agenda item and stick to it.

5. Make sure that differences of opinion are respected, and try to prevent the ridiculing of an idea that may sound unconventional.

6. Make sure that the person with the most authority speaks last; this will keep him or her from inhibiting openness. Nobody likes to disagree with the boss.

7. Last but not least, make sure someone is responsible for recording a list of action directives and distributing them at the close of the meeting or soon afterwards. These action directives should specify the responsibilities each person has been given and the agreed upon deadlines that resulted from the meeting. Distributing these to everybody will clarify and pinpoint accountability.

It's frustrating to walk out of a long, tedious meeting and hear key people saying, "Now, what is it that we're supposed to do?"

To further improve your meetings, you might wish to use the following survey, Ingredients for an Effective Meeting.

Action Tool: Ingredients for an Effective Meeting

The purpose of meetings is to inform, assign, decide, discuss, and solve problems. Effective and productive meetings are essential to the successful functioning of any company. Unfortunately, many meetings are too long with, oddly enough, little worthwhile participation and very little accomplished. As a result, people avoid attending them because they view them as a waste of time.

For meetings to be successful, they should be tightly structured and attendees must be given a chance to actively participate in an open forum.

The following survey assists you in evaluating how effective your meetings are and which ingredients are being used and which are missing.

Use this form on yourself. Answer the questions as you believe your employees would answer them. Remember, it's very important to be as objective as possible when completing the survey.

You should also have this survey completed by your employees, anonymously rating you in this area so that you are able to compare your perceptions to those of your employees.

Scoring Procedure

To determine how effective your meetings are, rate each factor based on the following scale:

1 = never   3 = half of the time

2 = sometimes 4 = most of the time

5 = always

	Never	Sometimes	Half of the Time	Most of the Time	Always

1. An agenda is prepared in advance and distributed in sufficient time prior to the meeting   1 2 3 4 5

2. All presentation material and equipment are prepared in advance   1 2 3 4 5

3. Attendees come prepared with reports and necessary materials   1 2 3 4 5

4. The meeting environment enables everyone to hear, see, and sit in comfort 1 2 3 4 5

5. Arguing for personal benefit is avoided 1 2 3 4 5

6. Positions are presented rationally as opposed to emotionally   1 2 3 4 5

7. All attendees have the opportunity to express their views before decisions are made   1 2 3 4 5

8. Persons having power and authority do not inhibit honest communication   1 2 3 4 5

9. Conflicts are not avoided   1 2 3 4 5

10. Differences of opinion are expected and respected   1 2 3 4 5

Subtotal: _____

	Never	Sometimes	Half of the Time	Most of the Time	Always
11. The same ideas are not gone over and over again	1	2	3	4	5
12. All attendees participate during some portion of the meeting	1	2	3	4	5
13. Someone is responsible for ensuring that all attendees have an opportunity to speak	1	2	3	4	5
14. Attendees are not fearful of having their views misquoted or misused	1	2	3	4	5
15. Interruptions are not allowed except for an emergency	1	2	3	4	5
16. Discussions remain focused and do not become tangential or irrelevant	1	2	3	4	5
17. Attendees are expected to stay the full length of the meeting	1	2	3	4	5
18. Latecomers are held accountable for their tardiness	1	2	3	4	5
19. Those who are required to attend the meeting and do not do so are held accountable for their absence	1	2	3	4	5
20. Someone is responsible for recording and distributing a list of action directives	1	2	3	4	5

Total: _____

Scoring Guide

Add up the scores for each factor and divide by 20 to determine your meeting-effectiveness score.

Interpretation Key

Check your score against the following scale:

1.0–1.5 = very poor meeting skills

1.6–2.5 = poor meeting skills

2.6–3.5 = average meeting skills

3.6–4.5 = good meeting skills

4.6–5.0 = excellent meeting skills

"WHO SHOULD SOLVE THIS PROBLEM?"

 I am really disgusted. We have so many unresolved problems. It's the same stuff all the time. The other managers are fed up with this as well. Unless the president of the company gets his act together, he's going to find a lot of us gone. I can't believe that the president of the company doesn't solve these problems. Do you think he's just inadequate or what?

A: It does sound as if you and your management peers are having a problem. But since you can't fire the president, the only practical approach is to look to yourselves for improvement. I'm going to assume that at least some of the problems you're having are with your subordinates, or with each other, or with management procedures, or with company direction.

You're adults. Why can't you tackle these difficulties? Why can't you try to identify a problem, decide on a solution, and implement it? Do you think your president would approach the problem any differently?

Too often, managers are waiting for big daddy to come in to rescue them. Too often, managers act like helpless victims who cannot think strategically.

My questions to you would be, "What would you do if you owned the business? What would you do to solve these problems?"

Now before you discount my words with "You don't understand how it is here," let me tell you that few presidents would turn down a clear statement of a problem accompanied by one or more possible solutions.

Have you considered that maybe the president doesn't know what to do about some problems? Maybe he's human. Maybe he has limitations like the rest of us. Maybe he's overwhelmed. Maybe he's waiting for one of the managers to step forward and solve the problem.

The problem is not that managers take too much initiative. Most often they take too little. I often advise managers to say, "I was thinking that somebody should do something about this problem, and then I realized 'I' was somebody."

"MY DOOR IS ALWAYS OPEN."

 I was just hired as a manager of a medium-size company. During my first day on the job, the personnel director took me to meet the president. The president shook my hand firmly and told me, "My door is always open." He seemed serious when he said, "If you have any problems at all, come and see me." Should I take him up on it?

A: Some presidents make this little speech because they think it's good for morale but don't mean it at all. If you pursue the invitation of this personality type, don't be surprised if he acts annoyed and asks you, "Why are you coming to me with this?"

Then there is the second type of president. He thinks he should be available to any employee who wants his ear. He doesn't want to lose touch with his employees. He is overaccessible and spends large chunks of his time playing daddy to his employees. (As a result, he may not pay enough attention to charting the company's course and steering the company ship.) This president is too paternalistic to be of real help.

The third type of president takes his job seriously and doesn't want his time taken up with issues that don't affect the larger picture. If there is a significant problem, he'll want to know about it; otherwise, he'll expect his staff to handle it.

Going to see the president is not a great idea. The person you should talk to is the manager to whom you report. It is *his* job to give you the tools, both human and material, to get your job done, *his* responsibility to give you the information you need, and *his* function to keep you motivated and fulfilled. That's what *he* gets paid for.

If this doesn't work (after you've tried several times), take the president up on his offer. Try to catch him at the beginning or end of the workday. You'll have more of his ear and his heart then.

"I WANT TO SHOW CONCERN."

 I get the distinct impression that our employees believe that our company and its managers look down upon them and don't value their contributions to our company. What can we say to our employees to combat this impression?

A: I'm glad you're concerned with this problem. Without a doubt it is affecting your productivity and profits. Here are a number of nice gestures that legitimately demonstrate warmth and regard for employees:

1. Enclosing a personalized thank-you letter to the employee in the pay envelope for a job well done
2. Using the company newsletter to promote communication and goodwill
3. Employing company bulletin boards to feature photographs of departmental accomplishments
4. Sending birthday cards and thank-you cards upon the anniversary of employment
5. Using the company intercom prior to a holiday to extend wishes to all employees for a happy holiday
6. Holding several company social events each year (e.g., picnic, Christmas party)
7. Posting awards for cost reductions, helpful suggestions, increased productivity, and other positive efforts
8. Holding employee-recognition events honoring employees for outstanding service
9. Taking small groups of employees out to dinner to express appreciation for their daily devotion to their tasks
10. Inviting employees once a year to the home of the chief executive officer or the supervisor or both
11. Sending flowers to the hospital when an employee is ill
12. Visiting the hospitalized employee more than once when there is an extended illness (try not to discuss work while you're there)

Chapter Three

IMPROVING SUPERVISION

Introduction

A manager is given an awesome amount of responsibility. If he has ten employees and each one earns $20,000 to $30,000 annually, the company has in effect given $200,000 to $300,000 to that manager at the beginning of the year and said, "Here, take this money. Go spend it on human assets and achieve the desired result for the company."

It is therefore critical that the manager have expertise in a great variety of areas including hiring, orienting, and training employees, delegating responsibility, ensuring accountability and productivity, and managing time. The list goes on.

Most managers are poorly equipped to perform the many tasks that are part and parcel of their everyday work life. The fault for this lies most often with the company employing the manager. As a result of inadequate apprenticeship and formal education, managers are forced to gain the knowledge they need on their own, and they do their best to do so. Managers, however, who wish to be good supervisors must keep in mind that there is no substitute for knowledge of management techniques and for their careful application. This chapter is about that knowledge and perspective.

"WE KEEP HIRING
THE WRONG PEOPLE."

Q: We have great difficulty in finding good employees for the positions we have available. We interview until we're blue in the face, but we find that many times our judgment has been incorrect. What are we doing wrong?

A:
You can improve your skills by reading books on interviewing, but they often fail to include guidance on matching the personality to the job.

People do tend to fall into vocational groupings. Some like to work with people (a salesman or a social worker); some with ideas (a scientist or a writer); some with numbers (an accountant or a statistician); some with machines (a mechanic or a TV repairman). Some do well working as part of a team, some in solitude. Some people are detail-oriented while others deal better with the whole picture. Some people can effectively handle many different problems simultaneously, while others would become overwhelmed by them.

It is true that people don't always fall purely into one category, but they do display patterns. What you want to find is someone whose personality preferences are the same as the requirements of the job. You want to go with the grain of the person you employ and not against it. For example, a sales position would best be served by a person who is extroverted, verbal, persuasive, likeable, and persistent.

One means of determining personality preferences is to find out what the candidate likes to do in his free time. When there are no restrictions, personality patterns become more evident. For example, the extrovert will be active in clubs and civic life. The introvert will spend the weekends reading. Another method is to ask which functions the candidate liked or disliked at the previous place of employment.

On occasion, you may have no choice but to fill a position with someone who is, in a sense, a square peg in a round hole. Only do this temporarily.

Before interviewing candidates, list the personality requirements of the job and find someone who is a personality match. For example, if you were searching for a vice-president of production, your personality requirements might include: strong communicator and leader, firm type, not wishy-washy, take-charge person, eye for detail, doesn't shoot from hip, good motivator, and ability to deal with many problems simultaneously. If you don't do this, you may end up hiring a person with a technical personality for a sales position, and you may find him tinkering with the computer instead of making his sales calls.

"WHAT ARE THE MOST IMPORTANT QUALITIES?"

 We are currently considering candidates for an important management position. We have three people we are seriously considering. For what traits do you think we should be looking?

A: As far as I am concerned, the most important quality to look for in a manager is judgment. This is hard to define and very difficult to teach.

Some will call it common sense, but as we all know, common sense is not so common. It is the ability to view a situation, examine its factors, consider the short-range and long-range effects, and then make a decision that is likely to be a good one (not always a good one, mind you, for perfection is not to be found in any person or creation).

I would also look for a person who knows when he doesn't know. This quality was somewhat humorously discussed during a lunch I recently attended. A member of British royalty was describing a world leader she had known for many years. She whispered to me, "He's not very smart, you know, but he's smart enough to surround himself with people who are."

Finally, I would want someone who is gifted with people, someone people trust and respect and who promotes goodwill. There is just no getting away from it: We make our fortunes with people. The toughie image really only works in James Cagney movies.

"I DIDN'T GET
TO KNOW
THEIR NAMES."

 Our company is having such a severe problem with turnover that before I get to know some of our employees, they are already gone. I come into the department and say, "Where's Terry?" The answer is, "She's gone." I ask, "Where's Cindy?" "She left last Friday. She didn't even take her things." "Well, what about David?" "David's leaving at the end of the month" is the reply. I can't tell you how many problems this causes us. We figure it takes new employees between three to six months to learn their jobs. In the interim they make lots of mistakes and we have all kinds of problems with credit, shipments, and unhappy customers. Why is this happening and what can we do about it?

A: In some situations, employees are not being paid enough to support themselves. They take low-paying jobs merely as a stopgap to tide them over until they can find something better. Even in this low-compensation environment, employers (such as your company) should try to create opportunities for employees to earn more money. This could be by:

1. Consolidating hours given to several workers and giving them to one person, who now has a livable income and possibly some employee benefits he did not have before
2. Offering additional compensation for taking on more responsibility, such as, "If you would take on the task of plant security, I think we could pay you a bit more"
3. Offering incentives for bringing in customers

In my opinion, however, the monetary dimension is not the greatest cause of employee turnover. Most often, it is the employee's perception of how he is treated that causes the employee to leave. The person generally credited with the reason for this exit is the immediate supervisor. Frequently, there are specific complaints about the supervisor's style.

Most repugnant to employees are supervisors who do the following:

1. Criticize them in public
2. Speak to them with sarcasm
3. Insult them personally
4. Exaggerate employee faults
5. Blame employees for their own shortcomings
6. Treat employees like children
7. Put employees in no-win situations
8. Yell at employees
9. Judge employees without giving them the opportunity to defend themselves
10. Complain about employees no matter how hard they try

11. Falsely accuse employees of crimes they did not commit
12. Take credit that rightfully belongs to the employees
13. Display a gross lack of courtesy
14. Reveal by their actions that they believe all employees are either incompetent, lazy, or both
15. Continually threaten employees with dismissal
16. Display racial, ethnic, or sexual prejudice
17. Continually assign employees to tasks below their level of skill and ability
18. Hold employees responsible for situations that are beyond their control
19. Do not accept the unavoidable human error
20. Constantly remind employees of past failings

When employees begin to experience a few of the above behaviors, they try to ignore them at first. When their sense of self-respect and dignity becomes too offended, they will try to vent their feelings to others. They hope the situation will be rectified. If there is no one to talk to and the problem continues to occur, they begin to lose hope and start to look elsewhere. This process does not occur overnight and there are opportunities for conciliation if management becomes aware of the problem.

There are a variety of methods to determine if the aforementioned negative behaviors are occurring.

1. Conduct exit interviews with all employees who leave the company, asking them for their honest evaluation of your company and its managers. Assure them that there will be no negative consequences to their sharing this information with you. Be careful also not to lead the employee in the discussion or you will obtain unreliable data. (Ideally, the employee's direct supervisor does not conduct the exit interview.)

2. Conduct employee-attitude surveys at least once a year. Make sure that anonymity is carefully protected.
3. Conduct a supervisor review program where employees anonymously rate their boss.

An additional reason for employee turnover is the failure to provide employees with the necessary tools to get their job done. When employees aren't given the tools to do their job properly, they inevitably fail. When this occurs, the supervisors are often critical. The employees defend themselves by protesting that the correct resources were not provided. Often, employees are told to make do and stop making excuses. This response leaves employees frustrated and feeling that they have been falsely accused. Since the needed resources typically are not given to the employees, the failure occurs again and again, and the criticism is repeated in stronger and stronger terms. The employees, after a while facing this type of problem, do not just leave the company, they flee the company.

Reducing turnover might also involve boosting employee morale. See "Morale is poor and no one cares," pages 7–9, and "I need to increase productivity," pages 15–16. Reducing turnover also involves making sure the right people are hired in the first place. See "We keep hiring the wrong people," pages 75–77.

"I WASN'T TOLD WHERE THE BATHROOM WAS."

 When I first started working here, they showed me where my desk was and introduced me to my new boss. She shook my hand, plunked down a huge pile of papers, and said, "Here, get started on this." She didn't reappear for three days. I didn't even know where the bathroom was, never mind how to do what she expected me to do. I don't want this to happen to others, so I've now become the welcoming committee. I want new employees to start off on the right foot. I know there is information I should be giving them about their job and the company, but I have a gnawing feeling that I'm leaving out really important facts. Please suggest a good way to do this.

A: Unfortunately, your early experiences at your company happen to many people. As bizarre as it may sound, some employees are never even told who their boss is. I know this to be true because I've asked employees the following question many times: "Who do you report to?" And not infrequently the response is, "Uh...uh..., I really don't know. Jimmy gives me work, Lucinda does too, and the clerical pool asks me to help them out from time to time."

A proper orientation to new employment is not only an act of courtesy, it also greatly reduces the learning curve of new employees, reduces mistakes, reduces waste of other people's time, and enhances efficiency and productivity. Employee orientation should be an automatic event rather than a "When we get around to it, we'll talk to her" routine.

Proper orientation includes two presentations: an orientation to the company and an orientation to the department, including the specific position that the new person will be taking.

An orientation to the company should include the following:

1. Welcoming the employee (stating length of employment, if temporary)
2. Introducing (where possible) principals, management, and department heads
3. Explaining company history and future direction
4. Touring the facilities, including lunchroom and rest areas
5. Providing a copy of the employee handbook and reviewing it with the employee
6. Explaining management's concern with accountability, treatment of company property, and employee fulfillment
7. Explaining the company's concern with cost reduction, profit improvement, and the quality of labor provided by the employees

8. Listing of resources, both human and material, available to the new employee both within the company and external to the company
9. Reviewing the company's employee-benefits program, including medical, hospitalization, dental, and life insurance programs, and pension/profit sharing plan
10. Reviewing company internal and external publications including company brochure
11. Explaining the chain-of-command policy and company-organizational chart
12. Explaining the company's disciplinary and grievance procedure
13. Reviewing the company's vocational and personal counselling policy, if one exists
14. Explaining the company's layoff and recall procedure
15. Reviewing employee-recognition events and programs
16. Reviewing the company's education and tuition-reimbursement policy
17. Explaining the company's health, emergency, and accident-reporting procedure
18. Explaining the company's fire and disaster procedure
19. Reviewing the policy on personal use of the telephone
20. Reviewing the company's social groups

An orientation to the specific department the person will be working in and the specific position should include:

1. Introduction to the direct supervisor and supervisory procedures
2. Introduction to peers and subordinates
3. Review of the department history and scope of operation
4. Explanation of the direction the department is taking

5. Review of the specific written job description
6. Review of the department's organizational chart
7. Tour of the department's facilities
8. Review of the work hours, lunch time, rest breaks, and overtime needs
9. Explanation of work-recording procedures
10. Review of wage and salary program for the position, including career path
11. Review of the company's employee-review procedure and schedule, salary increases, performance bonus, incentive pay, and Christmas bonus
12. Review of pay deductions, pay periods, and company cashing of checks
13. Review of promotion opportunities
14. Review of policy on reporting lateness and absences
15. Review of expected civic responsibilities
16. Availability of clerical assistance
17. Procedure on mail delivery and collection
18. Tour of specific work area, description of tools to be used, and selection of desk supplies
19. Review of policy on moonlighting
20. Review of company-paid subscriptions/library
21. Review of compliance with federal and state laws
22. Review of training program for the position and the training schedule

This list, of course, could be three times as long, but if you and the employee's supervisor-to-be will cover these subjects, you'll be well on your way to having a well-oriented employee.

"WHAT CAN I EXPECT FROM MY EMPLOYEES?"

 I expect my employees to come to work on time and not ten minutes late. I expect them to be working and not discussing the latest movie. I expect them to be tidy and not sloppy. When I raise these issues, they look at me with amazement. Have these things become too much to ask of employees? I can't believe it!

A: Frankly, I think you're asking too little. If your employees give you a surly response on the points you mention, I suggest you tell them, "I don't know how our company is going to live without you, but starting this Monday we're going to give it a real try." Adherence to basic work rules and standards should certainly be within the realm of your expectations.

The truth is that you need much more from your employees. And your question reveals that you need to increase your expectations rather than question your existing ones. As a manager, you should expect your employees to be committed to your department and to care about their work. You should expect them to give you their eyes, their ears, and most of all, their brains.

If you have ten people working for you, you should have ten minds generating ideas and solutions. If you have a thousand workers, then you should have as many of them as possible thinking about the company's problems as they drive home. The combined brainpower of your entire staff can be amazing. If you act like you expect your employees to give you their best efforts, they will; but in order to achieve this, they must believe that you are exerting similar efforts on their behalf.

"MY SUPERVISORS AREN'T ON MY SIDE."

 Q: I have six supervisors working for me. From my viewpoint, all of them are much too friendly with the men they supervise. They almost always take the side of the men rather than that of the company. Somehow my supervisors have allied themselves with their employees as opposed to supporting me. Why does this happen and what should I do?

A: I call this the It's Easy for You to Say; I've Got to Work With Them Syndrome. Most people want and need the love and approval of others. Some supervisors carry this too far. They want to receive love and approval from the people they work with as well as from family and friends.

They want to have a pleasant social environment on the job. They don't want employees to be angry with them, so they refrain from disciplining employees and, in effect, become one of the guys.

In other situations, supervisors align themselves with their employees when they feel that management is either unreasonable or incorrect.

In either case, you need to make clear to the supervisors you employ that you are paying them to supervise; if they wish to abdicate that function, they may, but the cost to them will be a reduction of their salary by at least $10,000 annually.

Also inform your supervisors that love and approval come most appropriately from spouses and friends, and not from one's employees.

You also owe it to yourself to ask them about the quality of your relationship with them and how it can be improved. I've got a feeling you'll find a lot of gripes, and some of them may be legitimate.

"I TOLD YOU
THIS WAS YOUR
RESPONSIBILITY."

Q: I asked one of my employees if he had finished an important project. He said, "No," and I asked, "How come? I told you this was your responsibility." He answered, "I was at meetings all day." I was very disappointed and said, "You should have finished the work!" and walked out the door. What can I do to prevent this kind of situation from recurring?

A: You may be experiencing what I call the Too Much, Too Little Syndrome. This occurs when a manager gives an employee too much work and too little prioritization.

When bosses give out work, they estimate how long the task will take and assess whether the employee can handle it with his or her existing work load. Sometimes, however, the manager's estimates are inaccurate. A manager may ask, "How long will it take to finish this? Two hours?" If the employee responds, "I'll be lucky to finish it in six hours!" the manager must try to reevaluate the difficulty of the task. Sometimes the manager misassesses the employee's current work load and the time required to complete the new assignment, and therefore he assigns too much work to be completed in too little time.

The solution to the Too Much, Too Little Syndrome has three parts:

1. Ask employees to list all the tasks you have assigned them to complete.
2. Have employees estimate the time each task requires.
3. Tell employees to present the lists to you so you can assign a priority to each task.

Instruct employees that when they are in doubt about how to spend their time, they should bring their questions to you for a decision. Additionally, managers would be well-advised to keep individual employee work sheets where they record the major assignments given to each employee. This will help the manager to assign work, maintain accountability, and distribute the work load both effectively and fairly.

"WHO'S ON FIRST?"

 Around here, all you hear is, "I wasn't supposed to do that"; "That's not my job!"; "What
are you looking at me for?"; "Why didn't you
take care of this?" Abbott and Costello must
have written our lines. People are fighting and
arguing. What can we do?

A: Fortunately, the answer to your problems is a simple management tool, a job description. It sounds like everyone who works at your company can use one. The job description simply lists what responsibilities each person has and what tasks he performs. Doing a job description for each person will clarify in writing whether George is responsible for shipping or Lou is. It also promotes accountability. People will no longer be able to say, "I didn't know that was my job."

When you write your job descriptions for the first time, you'll find duplication of effort (two people doing the same task), and you'll find areas where no one is responsible for the task. You may even decide that you want to change things around a bit and give Bob the task that Laura is now doing because you think Bob will do it better.

Below are instructions on how to create a job description:

1. Write down each action that the person doing that job would be required to do. To facilitate this process, a list of action verbs for job descriptions is included at the end of this section. For example, using the action verb *design*, the job might require that the employee:

- *Design* new patterns for the fall and spring lines
- *Design* the cover for the annual report
- *Design* the electronic controls for all new machines

As you review the action verb list, ask yourself if a particular action verb applies to the job or position description you are writing. For example, you might take the action verb *monitor* and say to yourself, "Does this position require monitoring?"

2. Ask the employee who is doing that position to list all of the tasks he currently performs. This will help you enlarge your list. This will also aid you

in removing those tasks that the employee should not be doing.

3. Prioritize the tasks with an A, B, C, or 1, 2, 3, rating system in terms of importance. This will convey a sense of priority to the employee.

4. Place a time frame next to each task to give the employee an idea of the amount of time he should be spending on it.

5. Add a section for goals in which you delineate special objectives for the coming quarter, for the next six months, and for the end of the year. For example, a goal might be to remove all unutilized equipment from the plant floor, or to establish a new filing system for the accounting department, or to learn the software program for inventory control. Don't forget to include some delineation of the necessary actions required to accomplish these goals.

Following is a list of action verbs that can be used for writing job descriptions.

Action Tool: Action Verbs for Job Descriptions

ACT	CONDUCT	EVALUATE
ADMINISTER	CONSULT	FOLLOW UP
ADVISE	CONTROL	FORECAST
AID	COORDINATE	FORMULATE
ANALYZE	CREATE	IDENTIFY
APPRAISE	CRITIQUE	IMPLEMENT
APPROVE	DECIDE	INFORM
ARRANGE	DEFINE	INITIATE
ASSESS	DELEGATE	INNOVATE
ASSIST	DESIGN	INTERPRET
ASSURE	DETERMINE	INVESTIGATE
ATTEND	DEVELOP	LEAD
AUDIT	DIRECT	LEARN
AUTHORIZE	DISSEMINATE	MAINTAIN
CARRY OUT	DOCUMENT	MANAGE
COLLABORATE	ENSURE	MODIFY
COMMUNICATE	ESTABLISH	MONITOR
COMPARE	ESTIMATE	NEGOTIATE

ORGANIZE	RECEIVE	SELECT
ORIGINATE	RECOMMEND	SUBMIT
PARTICIPATE	REFER	SUPERVISE
PLAN	REPORT	TEST
PREPARE	RESEARCH	TRAIN
PRESIDE	RESOLVE	VERIFY
PROBLEM SOLVE	REVIEW	WRITE
PROMOTE	SCHEDULE	
PROVIDE FOR	SEARCH	

"I HAVE TO
DO IT MYSELF."

 I manage three departments. I am always exhausted. My boss says it's my fault because I don't delegate more. I've tried, but the employees fail and jobs end up back in my lap. What can I do?

A: Let me tell you a story. A president called in a vice-president. "Harry," he said, "I want you to take care of the expansion. I know it's going to cost a million dollars, but I want you to take care of it. I don't want to be bothered with it."

The vice-president nodded. The president then said, "But I want you to check with me on a daily basis."

The vice-president looked totally confused. After he left, I said, "Do you think Harry understood what you said?" The president replied, "Of course he did. Do you want me to call him back in?" And he did. "You understood what I just told you, didn't you?" he inquired.

The vice-president hesitated and then said, "I don't know if you really want me to take care of it or if *you* are really going to be in charge."

This example illustrates just one of the potential pitfalls of faulty delegation. Perhaps you are giving responsibility without giving authority.

Other rules to keep in mind when delegating responsibility are:

- Choose a capable candidate.
- Train him or her adequately.
- Don't keep key factors confidential. Either trust the person or don't give him the job.
- Be accessible for questions.
- Monitor the performance without smothering the performer.

And last but not least, try not to get jealous, try not to feel insecure. If the delegatee does his job well, it will be to your credit and should not be viewed as a threat. If, on the other hand, you feel this worry because you're not doing your own job properly, I'd recommend that you concern yourself with your performance and not his.

If you wish to determine how well you delegate, use the following evaluative survey, Do's and Don'ts of Delegation.

Action Tool: Do's and Don'ts of Delegation

Delegation is a significant management function. An employee becomes a manager to supervise and coordinate the work of others besides carrying out some of his own specific work functions.

To be effective in a role as manager, the manager must delegate effectively as many functions as possible or he will not have sufficient time to supervise and coordinate his people to ensure that they are doing their jobs well.

The purpose of this survey is to assist managers in determining how well they delegate so that they can improve their skill and make their work more manageable.

Use this form on yourself. Answer the questions as you believe your employees would answer them. Remember, it's very important to be as objective as possible when completing the survey.

You should also have this survey completed by your employees, anonymously rating you in this area so that you can compare your perceptions with those of your employees.

Scoring Procedure

To determine effectiveness in delegation, rate each factor based on the following scale:

1 = never   3 = half of the time

2 = sometimes 4 = most of the time

5 = always

	Never	Sometimes	Half of the Time	Most of the Time	Always
1. Selects tasks that are appropriate for delegation	1	2	3	4	5
2. Selects subordinates who are most capable of handling the particular task	1	2	3	4	5
3. Explains the assignment thoroughly to the delegatee	1	2	3	4	5
4. Makes certain the delegatee understands the assignment	1	2	3	4	5
5. Makes certain the delegatee understands the specific performance level expected	1	2	3	4	5
6. Gives the delegatee the necessary information needed to carry out the assignment	1	2	3	4	5
7. Gives the delegatee any training that is necessary	1	2	3	4	5
8. Gives the delegatee a realistic time frame for completing the assignment	1	2	3	4	5
9. Gives the delegatee sufficient authority to get the job done	1	2	3	4	5
10. Gives the delegatee sufficient human and material assistance to carry out the assignment	1	2	3	4	5

Subtotal: _____

	Never	Sometimes	Half of the Time	Most of the Time	Always
11. Explains to the delegatee which additional resources are available, internal and external to the company	1	2	3	4	5
12. Establishes with the delegatee the frequency and type of progress reporting expected	1	2	3	4	5
13. Introduces the delegatee to appropriate personnel, explaining that authority has been transferred to him	1	2	3	4	5
14. Monitors the delegatee's work frequently	1	2	3	4	5
15. Is accessible to the delegatee if assistance is needed	1	2	3	4	5
16. Allows the delegatee a certain amount of flexibility in personal style and methodology	1	2	3	4	5
17. Allows the delegatee to make mistakes but expects him to learn from them	1	2	3	4	5
18. Critiques delegatee's performance periodically and offers helpful hints	1	2	3	4	5
19. Gives positive reinforcement to the delegatee throughout the assignment	1	2	3	4	5
20. Gives the delegatee proper public credit when appropriate	1	2	3	4	5

Total: _____

Scoring Guide

Add up the scores for each factor and divide by 20 to determine how well the manager delegates.

Interpretation Key

Check your score against the following scale:

1.0–1.5 = very poor delegation skills
1.6–2.5 = poor delegation skills
2.6–3.5 = adequate delegation skills
3.6–4.5 = good delegation skills
4.6–5.0 = excellent delegation skills

"I GET ALL
THE PROBLEMS."

 I am a very busy man, but even so, my employees come running to me with every little problem. The door to my office practically looks like the box office at a hit movie. You'd think they could take a little responsibility. They're like a bunch of children. What should I do?

A: Make certain that you are not part of the problem. Some managers punish their employees for showing initiative. They attack with "Who told you to do that?" or "Why didn't you consult with me first?" This tendency causes employees to ask endless questions.

Other managers are so critical when a mistake is made that employees learn to bring all decisions to them in order to avoid getting zapped.

If you are not doing either of the above, then I suggest that you convene small meetings and make clear to your employees that you expect them to:

1. Anticipate problems and attempt to solve them
2. Make decisions on the job (appropriate ones of course)
3. Act without need of constant direct guidance
4. Establish procedures, methods, and techniques that keep problems to a minimum
5. Seek opportunities to improve systems and procedures

Place a sign on your desk that reads, WHAT CAN YOU DO TO SOLVE THIS PROBLEM? and show it to your employees every time they bring you a problem that you believe they should be solving. Explain to your employees that they get paid not only for performing a task but also for thinking about it. If they disagree, tell them you will have to consider replacing them with people who are problem solvers and decision makers.

"NOBODY EVER TOLD ME."

 Q: I called in one of my employees the other day to ask him why he had left the plant even though he knew the generator had broken down. His reply was, "Nobody ever told me that generator was my responsibility." I got the same answer when I asked our engineer why two of our most important machines weren't working. What kind of response is this?

A: Their response could be genuine or it could be a manipulation.

It could be genuine because when we give out jobs to people we rarely give them a thorough job description (and I'm not referring to one out of a book). We rarely specifically explain what their responsibilities are. Typically, we don't lay out our expectations and convey to our employees what authority they have.

The result is that employees march to their own drummer, performing the tasks that they think are important and assigning a low priority to the rest. In other words, sometimes they really don't know their responsibilities; we haven't told them.

Sometimes, however, they do know, and they're playing a game. The game works like this: If they say, "Nobody ever told me," you can't *get* them. If this works, they win, and they get to play again.

How do you stop this manipulation? With a consequence. If you rant and rave when they play this game but nothing happens, they'll play the game again. If you respond with "Okay, but next time it happens, you'll receive a warning notice," the game abruptly ends.

We human beings are all alike. We become receptive to change if we have a powerful motivation to do so.

"THEY DO THINGS THEIR WAY."

 Q: We are in a very competitive business. We've been successful by giving our customers extra-special service. We've told our employees a hundred times that they must follow our customer service policies. When we stand on top of them, they do things our way. When we turn our backs, they do things their way. What should we do? We can't fire all of them.

A: Your first need is to sell your employees on your ideas of customer service. In order to do this, you need to write them down in a clear and logical fashion.

Your next step is to hold training meetings with your employees, explaining to them why company policies are important and the reasoning behind them. Cite specific examples and describe the effects of not following the customer service program.

Get the group to accept and adopt your ideas as their own. You may hear some very worthwhile ideas from your employees during these sessions. Where appropriate, integrate them into your manual.

When training is completed, give every employee a copy of the guidelines. Also, explain the consequences of not following them. Don't be harsh, but don't be weak either. Telling employees a hundred times is a sign that they're really not mindful of you and that your threats are not taken seriously. You need to change that image pronto.

This problem of noncompliance when you turn your back is most disturbing. What are the supervisors who report to you doing? Maybe you should tell them about the high salaries and excellent benefits your competition is offering.

"IT'S YOUR JOB
TO KNOW, IDIOT!"

 I supervise an infuriating manager who is in a responsible position. When I ask him a question, he very often answers, "I don't know." I feel like yelling at him, "What do you mean you don't know? It's your job to know, idiot!" Sometimes, I want to kill him. What do you think?

A: First, homicide is very messy and prison is boring. Second, calm down. You're right. It is his job to know. Many people don't realize that a significant part of their job is providing information, even if this means going out of their way to get it.

There are certain facts you can always expect your managers to know, among others: what their departments are producing, what their costs are, and what their people are doing.

You should inform your staff that if they are faced with a situation for which they cannot avoid saying, "I don't know," they should follow the comment with "I'll get you the information," and give themselves a deadline for producing the answer. They need to realize that you are not making idle chatter. You need the answer.

Sometimes when employees say, "I don't know," they are saying, "It's not my job to know," or "I'm too busy to find out," or "Why are you bothering me with this inconsequential question?" In all three cases they are conveying an "I-don't-care" attitude. When this happens frequently, the response spawns anger and hostility.

It is also true that some neurotics have adopted "I don't know" as a passive-aggressive strategy for driving other people up a wall. When confronted and questioned as to whether this is their intention, they reply with "I don't know," of course.

Employees who frequently respond with "I don't know" should receive the necessary orientation and training. If this doesn't solve the problem, seriously consider the possibility of giving another employer the opportunity to take advantage of the "I don't know" employee's services.

"NO ONE IS IN CHARGE."

Q: I heard you being interviewed on a radio talk show and you mentioned that many times when two people are in charge of something it's almost as if no one is in charge. What did you mean by that? I am asking because another manager and I are in charge of a lot of things together.

A: Dual responsibility for a single function is like two people holding a baby: At best it's awkward, and at worst it's downright dangerous.

What kind of problems occur? Employees get torn between the priorities of manager A and manager B. Or they learn to play games like this: Friday morning when manager A makes a request, the employee says, "Oh, I can't do it. Manager B is keeping me busy." When manager B asks for work to be done, the employee says, "Oh, I'd love to do it, but I can't. Manager A has an important project he needs me to finish."

Sometimes, both manager A and manager B place purchase orders through the employee for the same needed item. The company finally receives two of the same item when it needs only one and then finds that it can't return the extra one.

Often, manager A will assume that manager B took care of it and vice versa. Important tasks can be overlooked and then the blaming process begins.

Finally, my years of consulting experience with many different managers, from those in multibillion-dollar companies to those in small family businesses, has taught me that in order for a project to succeed it must follow one person's vision. Without this, you can end up with a car company that sells overweight chickens and used ukuleles.

"DON'T DISCUSS
YOUR SALARY."

 Q: We're cutting costs, and I'm hiring new employees for less than I am paying my existing employees. I have informed the new hires that they are not to discuss their salaries with the other employees. What should I do if they violate this rule?

A: I suggest that you not make a rule that no one will keep.

Within the first weeks of employment, the new employee gets a total education from his peers. He not only finds out what salaries other people are receiving, he finds out what his supervisor is like and what the work expectations are at the company.

Forbidding a new employee to discuss salary is like saying to somebody, "Whatever you do, don't think of white elephants." Suddenly the subject of white elephants becomes an obsession.

In general, employers should understand that employees do talk and do compare notes. The bonus you give to Harry with strict warnings about secrecy eventually becomes known. The extra days off you give Judy providing she won't tell anybody becomes the subject of much analysis and conjecture. The promotion that is to be announced at the right time is common knowledge weeks before.

You would do well to remember the words of Benjamin Franklin, "Three may keep a secret, if two of them are dead."

Paying different salaries for the same job may also have legal ramifications, so check with your attorney to cover all bases.

"MY EMPLOYEES AND I ARE CLOSE."

 I believe in being close to my employees. We go out a lot together socially, and one of the managers who works for me is the godfather of my daughter. I think it's wonderful to have that kind of rapport, but the president of the company says I'm wrong. What's your opinion?

A: Your president is right, and you are playing with fire. How will you criticize someone you are about to go with on a two-week vacation? If the situation arises, how will you be able to fire your daughter's godfather?

You're making a mistake and a bad one. Employees who become too friendly with their manager have been known to respond to discipline with "Hey, what's up with you? Is your wife giving you a hard time or what?"

More than that, they will resent you for doing the normal things managers do. They'll be thinking, "Look how stuck-up he gets when he's on the job." They will be contrasting your work behavior with your leisure-time behavior and feeling annoyed that you're not acting like the good guy they know you really are.

I advise my clients that socializing with employees is like using spices. Use a little and you'll be fine; use a lot and you'll ruin the whole thing.

Now, before I get a whole bunch of letters telling me of situations when socializing with employees has worked, let me tell you that I know it can. But my experience suggests that the odds are about a hundred to one against. It's a big risk and a poor bet.

"I WANT A S.W.A.T. TEAM."

 Q: This may sound silly, but I always admired the precision, coordination, and mutual helpfulness of the S.W.A.T. teams I've seen on television. Everybody knows what to do. There's no bickering. It functions like a smooth machine. I'd like to have that kind of team here in the office. How can I accomplish that?

A:
A good team is the result of a lot of work on everybody's part and building it does take some time, but do not allow this to discourage you. The rewards are well worth the investment. Team building is enhanced by the following:

1. *Having a good reason for having a team.* Too often, teams are assembled that should not exist. The task does not require a team. Or the team is too big and employees feel they could be elsewhere; "They don't need me for this." Teams should be as small as possible.

2. *The team mission must be viewed as significant.* The television example you give is a good one because their "raison d'être" is saving human life and preventing catastrophes, an obviously important objective. Your team has to have an important goal. If the mission is perceived by your troops as being trivial or inconsequential, the group will not coalesce around it. A strong team will only form around a strong goal.

3. *Choosing the team members carefully.* Try not to include show-offs, loudmouths, takeover or argumentative types. The team will be annoyed by them. They will slow progress and you will find the group resisting them. Also, they will create discontent.

4. *Choosing a capable leader and a good lieutenant.* Choose people who motivate others, people who can bring out the best in people, and people who are conflict solvers as opposed to conflict makers.

5. *Making sure that everybody knows what to do.* This is very important in two respects: (1) The mission or goal of the team is clearly laid out, and (2) everybody understands what his specific role and responsibilities are. This will prevent people from stepping on each other's toes and will encourage initiative and progress.

6. *Meeting regularly and often to discuss problems and brainstorm.* Team members are like links in a chain. If one link breaks, the whole chain is useless. Encourage the whole team to offer ideas and assistance to individual team members. Promote an open forum where employees feel free to share problems and accomplishments.

7. *Treating the team as an elite group.* Make membership in the team a privilege, not everyone can get in. Create interest in the team's progress throughout the company.

Do this correctly and S.W.A.T. teams will come to observe your team.

"I AM NOT A TRAINER."

Q: Our company is expanding very quickly, and we just hired over twenty new employees. I am responsible for training all of them, and although I'm not a professional trainer, I want to do a good job. Can you give me some guidelines to follow?

People in management positions frequently find themselves in the position of educator. Here are some of the basics to follow:

Encouragement

1. Do not say to an employee, "You mean you didn't know 'x' before?"
2. Tell the employee that you also did not know, but you learned.
3. Reward the employee for learning part of the task.
4. Display patience and an approving attitude to the employee.
5. Give the employee the impression that he can and will be successful at his task, explaining why this is so.

Orientation

6. Inform the employee of the importance of attending all the training sessions, or he may miss important information and the learning of crucial skills.
7. Inform the employee of your performance expectations (first week, first month, etc.).
8. Inform the employee of the deadline for complete mastery of the task.
9. Inform the employee of your expectation for speed.
10. Inform the employee of your expectation for accuracy.
11. Inform the employee of your expectation for quality.
12. Explain to the employee the consequences of poor performance to the operation.
13. Explain the dangerous portions of the job to the employee (if any).
14. Inform the employee of what procedures to use under an emergency situation.

Instruction

15. Give the employee enough time in initial and successive training sessions.
16. Give instructions in quiet locations, if possible.
17. Attempt to give the employee guidance, first on the most common occurrences, and second on occasional and infrequent occurrences involved in the task.
18. If the employee is experiencing difficulty, attempt to trace the specific obstacle and take steps to remedy it.
19. Do not assume the employee will necessarily learn in one or two sessions.
20. Where possible, give the employee written and illustrated instructions as well.
21. Give the employee assignments to master in the initial phase of training.
22. Criticize the employee first on the gross errors, then on the fine errors.
23. Prevent the employee from overloading his own system and setting unrealistically high standards.
24. Make sure the employee writes down instructions instead of leaving it to memory.
25. When explaining something difficult to the employee, have the employee repeat what you have said in his own words to check that he understands.
26. When teaching a skill through observation, make sure the employee can clearly see each of your actions.
27. Pose problems to the employee that he may encounter and ask the employee how he would handle it.
28. When asking questions of the employee, use mostly open-ended questions and not yes-no questions.
29. If you need to use any instruction booklets, make sure they are understandable; if not, possibly rewrite them or order better ones.

30. Give the employee immediate and constant feedback on how he is doing.
31. If the employee asks a question you cannot answer, tell the employee you don't know the answer but that you'll get the information.
32. When criticizing the employee, always give positive criticism first, then the negative criticism.

Language

33. Try not to use too much unfamiliar jargon in your training sessions.
34. Use language that fits the level of the employee's educational background.
35. Explain carefully the metalanguage that is necessary for the employee to know.

"THIS SEMINAR
SOUNDS GREAT."

Q: I constantly get mail promoting management seminars and cassette programs. These seminars aren't cheap but I think they are well worth the money. Don't you agree?

A: Caveat emptor, or "Let the buyer beware," applies quite pointedly. Here are some of my concerns.

Seminar promoters often vow to change employees in a dramatic way in a one, or two day period. This is fantasy and not reality. Thinking styles and behavior modes take a lot of time to change. As Mark Twain said, "Habit is not to be flung out of the window by any man, but coaxed down the stairs a step at a time."

If a seminar is worthwhile, it will give your managers a number of insights. This does not mean that they are going to run right back to the office and immediately put them into practice. A majority of those who attend seminars remain unchanged by their experience except for having some intellectual stimulation and acquiring new fodder for weekend conversations.

Many seminar programs are designed to appeal to a wide audience. The result is that much of their material is too general and hence difficult to apply.

Please don't get the impression that I am against seminars, because I am not. Here is realistic advice, however:

1. Don't expect sweeping changes. The alteration of even small habits requires a great deal of effort and cannot be accomplished overnight.
2. Make sure you get results from your expenditure by asking the attendee to report on the experience.
3. Consider in-house seminars. They're a lot more effective, can be tailored to specific needs, waste less time, and can even cost less. Often people return from boilerplate-type seminars with comments like these: "It was interesting but not really applicable to our situation," or, "Their ideas would work if you had a lot of money to spend."

To evaluate seminars you have attended or will attend, you might wish to use the following guide, Getting the Most From Seminars.

Action Tool: Getting the Most From Seminars

Many companies send their managers and employees to seminars to learn new and better skills. Often though, the seminar attendee returns to the job with very little gained though much money has been spent. If attending a seminar is approached in the proper fashion, the company funding the seminar may receive a higher return on its investment. Use the following guide to assist you in receiving the maximum benefit from seminars.

Before the Seminar

1. Interview the seminar leader to determine if subjects covered are appropriate.
2. Inquire if there is a money-back guarantee if not satisfied.
3. Inquire if handout materials are provided and what they are.
4. Inquire if the session is taped and if cassettes are available for purchase.
5. Make sure you prepare for the seminar by reading texts, setting objectives, and preparing questions.
6. Where possible, videotape or make an audio recording of any in-house seminar.

After the Seminar

7. Prepare and give a brief oral report describing the seminar to your immediate work group.
8. Prepare a list of behaviors or practices that you will adopt or refine as a result of attending the seminar.
9. Determine which behaviors others need to change in order for you to effect your own change. For example, you attended a time-management seminar and you

want a quiet time each day to do work that requires concentration. You will need to ask people who come to your office not to disturb you during specific times.

10. Enlist the aid of significant others around you in actively supporting the change. For example, insist that employees follow the chain of command so that there is less havoc, or avoid hallway conversations that dwell on issues that should really be covered in an organized meeting.

11. Verify after 30, 90, 365 days which behaviors or practices you have adopted or refined as a result of attending the seminar.

12. Place the seminar materials and cassettes in the company library for companywide use.

13. Try to become an expert in the given area. You could then become the resident trainer in the area. Over time and with additional study, you may become very knowledgeable in plant security, pollution avoidance, or inventory control, for example.

14. When possible, evaluate the effectiveness of the seminar immediately after the seminar has been given using a formal rating system.

"NO ONE IS HAPPY WITH EVALUATIONS."

Q: Our company has a formal employee-evaluation procedure. We do this once a year. For some reason, it doesn't turn out well for employees or managers. Everyone comes away unhappy. Can you give me some ideas for improvement?

A: The purpose of a performance evaluation should be to motivate employees by praising and reinforcing strengths, by pointing out weaknesses, *and* by helping employees overcome their inadequacies. Here are some specific approaches:

1. Make sure that evaluations reflect overall performance of the past year and not just the last week or two.
2. Make sure that performance is not judged on single events but on patterns of behavior.
3. Do not hesitate to give an employee a perfect rating in a particular area if he deserves it. It doesn't happen often, but it can. So don't be stingy.
4. Have each employee do the same evaluation on himself and compare the employee's and manager's results.
5. Develop specific strategies to help employees overcome their weaknesses. For example, a weak salesperson may need to be teamed up with a stronger one or may need to learn more about the product or service he is selling.
6. If any evaluation turns out totally positive or totally negative, throw it out, and start over. Chances are that the employee is neither an angel nor a devil.

To find out more about how to evaluate reliably, use the following checklist, Effective Performance Evaluations.

Action Tool: Effective Performance Evaluations

The purpose of a performance evaluation is to give feedback and improve performance. Two ways to use evaluations are to motivate by praising strengths and to improve by targeting weaknesses. This checklist provides specific tips and guidelines to assist you in making your performance evaluations more effective in improving employee performance.

1. Evaluations should not be used as a baseball bat to punish an employee.
2. Use the job description as part of the evaluation.
3. Use the given criteria, but if they don't express what you're concerned about, write your own comments. If you wish, add criteria.
4. The evaluation should reflect performance during the entire period, not only the last two weeks.
5. People hesitate to give bad scores. It is better to go through those bad moments than to live with an ongoing chronic condition for years.
6. If the evaluation is scored all bad or all good, you're either too severe or too gentle. There should be a distribution of scores.
7. Go over the evaluation with all your employees months in advance of the actual evaluation so that they are aware of what they will be evaluated on. Give them a copy.
8. Have the employee also do the evaluation on himself.
9. Have the director of personnel or the director of your department review the evaluation prior to your discussing it with your employee.
10. Agreement should be reached with the employee concerning problem areas. If you are not in agreement, find some way to prove that what you are saying is correct.
11. Be ready to provide positive and negative examples to back up what you say.
12. Let employees negotiate with you. There is no shame in changing your score.
13. Give the employee confidence that he can do better.
14. Remember, if the employee walks out demotivated, you haven't done it right.
15. Give the employee a copy of the evaluation to keep.
16. If an employee receives a poor evaluation, the employee should be reviewed each month until he receives a better one.

"WE DON'T ACHIEVE OUR GOALS."

 At the beginning of last year, we established goals for our sales department. We based these goals on the performance of other companies that are about our size. We didn't achieve these goals. We didn't even come close. The year before the same thing happened. This year when we handed out our goals, the sales force was snickering, "Why waste the paper? You know and we know that these goals will never be achieved. Why don't you stop kidding yourself?" I was embarrassed and angry. After I calmed down, I thought to myself, "They're right," but I don't know why they're right. Other people are succeeding. Why aren't we?

A: Goal setting is like any other skill. In order to do it well, you have to understand certain elements and then apply them. Some of these elements are:

• Goals should be developed based on the current ability and experience of your staff. Your expectations can and should include improving somewhat, but giant leaps happen more often in novels and films than they do in real life.

• Goals should not be "handed out" as you put it. They should be arrived at in the following manner:

1. Management selects a goal.

2. Employees select a goal.

3. They meet together, negotiate, strategize, and agree upon a realistic goal. Management, of course, has the final say, but by giving the employees the opportunity for input, the employees buy in to the goal. They also refine management's thinking. Being in the trenches all of the time, employees often know more about the obstacles that confront them than their bosses.

• Goals should be questioned, reviewed, and challenged. When an employee says he can improve his output by 50 percent, the question should be, "How?" Some employees feel put upon when asked this question, but don't worry, they'll live through it. Press on and ask, "How?" and "Why would this work?" Too often, goals are chosen out of thin air with no strategic plan concerning how they will be accomplished. These goals usually fall flat on their faces.

• Goals should be put in writing with specific, measurable milestones. The act of putting the goal onto a visual medium enhances its chances for realization.

• Big, ambitious goals should be broken into small, attainable goals. Increasing the company's sales by 100 percent is a big, ambitious goal. A smaller, attainable goal would be a 5 percent increase or a 10 percent increase. Along the way, there should be rewards and ways to reinforce positive, desired behavior. Huge goals seem overwhelming and unreachable. When faced with these, employees tend to give up before they start. "What am I trying for? I'll never make it!" Small successes motivate employees to continue to climb the hill.

• Use visual reminders when possible to highlight the goals and the progress made toward them. Signs, graphic representations, recognition devices, and letters are all good. And don't believe employees when they tell you that these things are unimportant to them. Just watch their eyes when you've posted something new on the bulletin board.

• Too often forgotten is the fact that goals have a price attached to them. If the current sales are $9 million, they will not magically become $11 million. There will be a cost. The cost might be more sales personnel, more advertising, and/or more operating personnel to handle the increase in work. The cost may be in more work hours. The cost may be in the de-emphasis of another product. The cost may be in priorities. There is always a cost in achieving any goal. There are two questions to ask: (1) What are the direct and indirect costs of achieving this goal? and (2) Are the company and employees willing to pay the costs?

Remember, effective planning will yield effective goals and effective goals will yield impressive results.

"WHAT ADVICE SHOULD I GIVE MY MANAGERS?"

Q: I was just promoted. I now have four fairly young managers under me. Each one has ten to twenty employees. They're all flying to New York next week for our annual meeting. I'm slated to give a seminar. What do you think are some of the important rules I should give them about management?

A: Here are a few to begin with:

- Don't speak critically about employee A to employee B. Employee A will find out eventually, and employee B will be wondering and worrying if the manager is talking about him to employee C.
- Don't tease employees about raises with comments like, "You guys are not going to have to worry about paying more taxes this year, are you?" Don't mock their job security with such remarks as, "We'll see you all on Monday. I mean, we'll see *some* of you back on Monday." Employees may laugh with the manager when he makes such joking statements, but inside they resent them and think they're cruel.
- Don't ever call employees nerds, drones, wimps, or jerks. This reprehensible custom is tasteless and alienates employees. It also causes a loss of respect from their supervisors.
- Take great pains to treat your employees equally. Rewards, bonuses, and promotions should be given with objectivity. Avoid favoritism and prejudice. Divide work evenly and listen to your employees. Managers can often discover ways in which they can improve from their employees.

The Golden Rule is an excellent guide for managers: Do unto others as you would have others do unto you.

"THERE JUST ISN'T ENOUGH TIME!"

Q: One of the problems I'm constantly having is time. We don't have enough of it. Neither I nor my employees are able to get our work done. Incompleted work spills over from day to day, week to week, and month to month. We are getting more and more behind even though we're all coming in earlier and leaving later every day. A couple of my employees feel that we aren't managing our time correctly. I don't think this is probable, but it is possible. Could you give some guidance?

A: If the work load is a reasonable one, then improved time management may very well be the answer to your problems. To effectively change how you and your staff manage time, these steps must be carefully followed:

1. Individual and company time-wasting behaviors must be identified. Much of the ineffective time use may stem from poorly organized company procedures, unclearly expressed goals, and inadequate or mis-communication. Effective time management must be an individual and company project. One hand cannot applaud.

2. An appropriate behavior-modification program must be instituted to ensure behavioral change. Many of us are well aware of some of our time wasters, yet we have not changed them. We tend to avoid making those changes for a few reasons, in fact, for the same reasons we waste our time:

   a. It's difficult.
   b. We procrastinate.
   c. We are not motivated enough.
   d. We are overwhelmed.

3. Change needs to be done systematically. First, you must log your tasks and the time spent on them. Second, you need to prioritize them. Third, you need to analyze your behavior in regard to each task. Fourth, you need to look at each holistically, the task and the time you spend in relation to yourself and your company's expectations.

4. You cannot make effective changes in behavior in a vacuum. Necessary changes must clearly be communicated to others, for very often it is the others that eat away at your time. The critical others in your work life must also learn to use their time effectively, for proper use of your time depends almost as much on them as on you.

5. For each behavior that is identified as a time waster, an effective and efficient behavior must be

sought to take its place. Specific improvements you may wish to make include cutting out unnecessary and repetitive paperwork, being more concise and clear in your communications, and being more organized and better prepared for meetings with only the essential people attending.

People say time is money, but in truth, no sum of money can buy even one more minute of time. It is by far our most valuable possession.

In order to determine how effectively you are using your time, I suggest you use the following Time-Management Evaluation.

Action Tool: Time-Management Evaluation

Managers need to manage their time more effectively because they are typically working against deadlines. Not managing time may lead to greater and greater tension, frustration, and conflict. The following survey will assist the manager in determining how well he manages his time and which behaviors need to change in order for him to manage time better.

To obtain a more objective evaluation on how effectively time is being used, the manager should have his employees and the supervisor above him complete the survey, rating the manager on his use of time.

First, use this survey on yourself, answering the questions as you believe your employees would answer them. Remember, it's very important to be as objective as possible when completing this survey.

Then you should have this survey completed by your employees, anonymously rating you in this area so that you can compare your perceptions with those of your employees.

Scoring Procedure

To determine how well you manage time, rate each factor using the following scale:

1 = never   3 = half of the time

2 = sometimes 4 = most of the time

5 = always

	Never	Sometimes	Half of the Time	Most of the Time	Always
1. Does not procrastinate	1	2	3	4	5
2. Delegates when possible	1	2	3	4	5
3. Knows when to say no to unnecessary requests	1	2	3	4	5
4. Plans work ahead carefully	1	2	3	4	5
5. Closes door to reduce drop-ins	1	2	3	4	5
6. Does not attend unnecessary meetings	1	2	3	4	5
7. Keeps unnecessary phone calls to a minimum	1	2	3	4	5
8. Does not indulge in unnecessary conversations	1	2	3	4	5
9. Keeps desk uncluttered	1	2	3	4	5
10. Is well-organized	1	2	3	4	5
11. Establishes goals	1	2	3	4	5
12. Keeps a log of daily activities	1	2	3	4	5
13. Prioritizes daily activities	1	2	3	4	5
14. Completes one activity at a time	1	2	3	4	5
15. Keeps to a schedule	1	2	3	4	5

Subtotal: _____

	Never	Sometimes	Half of the Time	Most of the Time	Always
16. Gets right to the point in conversation	1	2	3	4	5
17. Keeps memos, letters, and reports as brief as possible	1	2	3	4	5
18. Standardizes procedures when possible	1	2	3	4	5
19. Uses time spent waiting productively	1	2	3	4	5
20. Selects a quiet place when work requires concentration	1	2	3	4	5

Total: _____

Scoring Guide

Add up the scores for each factor and divide by 20 to obtain the level of time-management effectiveness.

Interpretation Key

Check your score against the following scale:

1.0–1.5 = very poor use of time

1.6–2.5 = poor use of time

2.6–3.5 = average use of time

3.6–4.5 = good use of time

4.6–5.0 = excellent use of time

Chapter Four

HANDLING CONFLICT

Introduction

More than any other force, excessive conflict can destroy a department or company. I emphasize the word *excessive* because some conflict is unavoidable and, in fact, may even be desirable. There is a natural tension between sales and operations, between unconventional and conventional thinkers, and between all the support departments that are vying for the same budgetary dollars. These are healthy conflicts and should not be discouraged.

Conflicts that arise out of resentment, jealousy, backbiting, gossip, or perceived insult are in a different category. These forms of conflict tend to fester and poison the hater and the hated. These destructive and often emotional battles must be dealt with. Innocent bystanders get drawn into them, and soon all sense of perspective is lost.

The concerned manager has an obligation to deal with conflicts that have an impact on the operation of the business. When John cannot sit next to Mary though functionally he should, when managers and their subordinates do not get along, when professional conflict makers cause unrest, it is time to deal with the problem.

In many companies, conflicts are considered taboo and not open for discussion. They are underground thoughts whispered about at the water fountain and in the parking lot. Undesirable conflict is like a time bomb waiting to go off. Find the conflict and deal with it before it causes irreparable damage.

"WHY DO WE HAVE TO CHANGE?"

Q: The new managers are much bigger risk takers than I am. I don't like to jump into things. Every time an issue comes up, they want to change things and I usually want them to remain the way they are. This causes us to argue constantly. Who is right?

A: Actually, none of you have an effective decision-making style. The new managers sound impulsive, while you sound paralyzed. Both approaches are extreme. What you both need is more information. Why do I say this? Here are some illustrations of how the problem works:

Let's say that the marketing manager suggests revising part of the product line and you are opposed because you are afraid the customers won't buy the new items. Your peer swears they will. How will you find out who is right? By getting information! Ask the customers if they will buy them. Don't worry. They'll tell you the truth.

The production manager wants the company to buy better machinery. You don't agree that the expenditure is worthwhile. Get some more information. Go to visit some companies where the proposed machinery has been in operation for several years. Then you'll have a better perspective.

Your company's sales manager wants the company to subsidize a new showroom in San Diego. You say it's much too expensive. He says it isn't. You go back and forth. There's no need for this argument. Get some more information! Call several real estate people in California.

Although some disagreements are differences of opinion, most of the time they are conflicting perceptions of fact, and there are definitely ways to find out what is fact and what isn't.

Many people are resistant to finding out whether their perceptions of reality are correct or not. They say insistently, "I know!" implying that this knowledge should be enough. They're offended that their views are even questioned. They do not wish to have an interactive discussion: They make pronouncements. They don't want to submit their beliefs to the acid test of truth.

When you have a disagreement about a decision, ask yourself, "How can I get more information about this subject?" The information yielded may make you comfortable enough to say yes, or it may compel your employees to say, "You know, maybe this isn't such a good idea after all."

"HE DOESN'T GET ALONG WITH OTHERS."

Q: I am in a difficult predicament. The manager of marketing who reports to me gets along well with me but poorly with the managers of my other departments. In my opinion, all of my managers are hardworking and dedicated. My marketing manager always views the other managers very critically. There is constant conflict between him and them. What should I do?

A: Explain to your marketing manager that:

1. One of the ways in which you evaluate your staff is by their ability to cooperate harmoniously with one another in achieving the company's objectives and goals.
2. Each manager plays a critical part in making things happen, and each link of the chain is important.
3. Internal dissension and discord that result in loss of motivation and productivity can pose a severe threat to the survival of the company in the long term.
4. Managers should view their peers in a positive manner as resources for problem solving and brainstorming.
5. A basic respect and regard for other employees, no matter what their station, is a prerequisite for effective work relationships and employment at your company.

Your marketing manager needs to be reminded, "Do not use a hatchet to remove a fly from your friend's head." If he can't learn this, forget the fly and use the hatchet on him.

"HE'S TRYING
HIS BEST."

Q: He's been with us for a year—a very long year. His subordinates don't respect him. I meet with him at least once a week to tell him what he's doing wrong. He thanks me and goes back and makes the same mistake in a different way. He's not getting the job done. I need to fire him, but he's got three kids and he's trying his best. I don't know what to do.

A: Are you torn between what's good for your business and what's good for this employee? Don't be. If it's not good for both, it's not good for either one.

Think about it. If you're unhappy with his performance, you'll show it in your face when you look at him; you'll show it in your tone when you speak to him; you'll reveal it in your conversation with other employees. "No, don't ask John to do that," you will say. Soon they'll come to understand that you have little confidence in John. This attitude will spread and he'll become a loser in everyone's eyes. Life will not be pleasant for him.

Ask yourself these questions also:

1. Does he have any future with the company?
2. Is it wise to keep this employee when his incompetence hinders the efforts of others and makes their lives more difficult?
3. Wouldn't it be better for him to find employment where his contributions will be valued?

There are many ways of looking at firing. One view, a favorite of mine, was described to me by an especially articulate client who is the president of a sizable corporation. He calls it *compassionate repositioning*.

"I WANT TO FIRE HER."

Q: I have an employee who goes too far. This woman comes in late and has terrible attendance. I'm convinced she's a pathological liar. She makes up stories about why she didn't get her work done that would be hilarious in a situation comedy but cause havoc in the office. She is constantly making mistakes and blaming them on others. I have to fire her, but I'm just not sure how to go about it.

A: Firing employees today is not as easy as it used to be. Dismissed employees have brought suit against their former employers and have won big judgments. All the same, inferior employees must be discharged and the best type of professional to consult on this type of problem is a labor attorney. But meanwhile, let me give you a few pointers that the professionals have given me.

It's important to create a "paper trail" in which you document the employee's unacceptable behaviors. The way to do this is to write a series of memorandums over a given period of time listing the offenses and how often they occur. These should be shared with the employee (some recommend that you have another manager present when you do this). You inform the employee that the memo will be inserted in her personnel file. You can also ask the employee to sign the memo indicating that she has read it and understood it. Every time the employee repeats the offense, you go through the same procedure.

When employee-evaluation time comes, you once again note your dissatisfaction in writing, and do not give the employee any raise other than a cost of living increase (if it is the company custom that you give this to everyone in the organization regardless of merit).

Be careful not to express dissatisfaction with the employee if you do not do the same with other employees who exhibit similar behavioral or performance problems.

Careful review should be given to the following areas:

1. An employee contract, if one was given
2. The company handbook, if it is specific about disciplinary or dismissal procedures
3. Any verbal commitment for long-term employment, if given

4. The disciplinary procedures used with other
employees versus this employee

A review with a competent labor attorney of this
entire subject will prove valuable to you in this and
other instances.

"I'M AFRAID
TO FIRE HER."

 I have an office manager whom no one can stand. She's rude to me and sarcastic with the other managers. On the other hand, she is very competent and is quite meticulous in doing her job well. I'd like to get rid of her, but no one knows as much as she does. I am afraid I would be lost without her. What should I do?

A: I have met this type of embittered and caustic employee before. She casts a gray pall over the office, and everybody who comes in contact with her comes away lashed by her tongue. Believe me, I know the type. Sometimes this person is not getting the cooperation she needs to get her job done, and sometimes she feels her efforts and achievements go unrecognized. More often, however, she just has an acidic personality.

My usual advice about this kind of chronic complainer is to get rid of her. Of course, first train others in her functions. You'll be surprised how well your company survives without her. You'll even find that you enjoy coming to work more, because you won't have to experience the frustration of listening to her unending list of grievances.

Morale, as we know, is a very important factor in the productivity of a company. My rule is quite simple. If you have people who by virtue of personality demoralize others, look for the earliest opportunity to get rid of them.

"HE'S CONSTANTLY CRITICIZING ME."

 I work with a peer who is constantly criticizing me and everyone else. He likes to show how knowledgeable he is and that he is the only guy who gets anything done around here. The boss laps it up, and the two of them have lengthy conferences discussing all the employees. This guy is hell-bent on climbing to the top over our bodies. What should we do?

A: This person is what I call a PCM—a professional conflict maker.

PCMs are very dangerous, not only to employees but to the entire company. They can create severe morale and credibility problems that eventually become productivity problems. They are not to be underestimated, for they can be cunning and vicious. They only flourish, however, in a situation in which the boss is a willing participant.

PCMs can often be defeated by their own methods. Consider the following strategies:

1. PCMs devote so much of their energies to criticizing other people's performance that they often neglect their own tasks. When your troublemaker does this, find subtle ways of pointing out his inadequacies to the right people.

2. PCMs tend to use distortions and lies to pit employee against employee, always assuming that the destructive seed they have planted will keep the parties apart. You and your co-workers must break this pattern. You must take care not to heed the PCMs' machinations. Instead, you should collaborate and share strategies in a common defense.

3. It is worth noting that professional conflict makers rarely confine their volleys to employees or peers. Their highly critical appraisals usually include disparaging remarks about the boss and his management style. At the appropriate time, you may want to share with your boss your concerns about the damage being done to his image by the PCM he has been trusting. By the way, bring along a witness or two to enhance your credibility. If you keep your remarks dispassionate, your boss will probably see the light.

A favorite true story concerns a client of mine: A manager became fed up with all the negative criticism he was getting from a PCM about his employees. He called everyone into a large room and said to the PCM, "Why don't you stand up and tell me those stories about Jim, Diane, and Lou one more time?"

"I CAN'T ARGUE WITH HIM."

 About a year ago, I recommended that my company hire a manager with whom I had previously worked at another company. We are now working together in the same department, but, boy, has he changed! I can't talk to him. Our discussions end up in screaming matches. I try to stay rational when he gets emotional, but it's very difficult to keep my cool. I don't know what to do.

A: The communication breakdown you are experiencing can be solved, but first you must insist that certain rules be followed:

> Rule one: Each party will be allowed to present his position fully. If either one is prevented from doing this because of constant interruptions, it will not be possible to resolve the issue.
>
> Rule two: Each person must finally accept and adopt the position of greatest logic, no matter who presented it. If one participant enters the discussion resolved to maintain his own viewpoint, no matter what evidence is presented to the contrary, the discussion will be in vain and may even serve to exacerbate matters.
>
> Rule three: Tantrums are unacceptable. If one participant has a tantrum, the other participant should leave the meeting until the offender behaves in a civil fashion.
>
> Rule four: Tangents are unacceptable. Ten different issues can't be discussed at one time. When tangential matters are brought up, the other participant should not allow the discussion to become deflected. He should refocus on the original issue, assuring the other participant that the other issues will be dealt with subsequently.

Sometimes the presence of a referee can be helpful. The referee's job is not to determine the right or wrong of each person's position, but to supervise the discussion and make sure no low blows or unfair blows are delivered. If, for example, party A says to party B, "You're yelling," and party

B says, "No, I'm not," the referee can give an unbiased perspective.

Additional guidelines for constructive fight styles can be found in *The Intimate Enemy*, by Dr. George R. Bach and Peter Wyden (New York: Avon Books, 1981).

If your peer doesn't respond in a cooperative fashion to the rules outlined above, forget your past relationship and go to a higher authority with your problem.

"HIS MIND
IS CLOSED."

 I am the vice-president of manufacturing, and I report to a chief executive who is the most closed-minded person I've ever met. His reply to just about everything is, "We've always done it this way, and if it worked the old way for the last forty years, it will work for the next forty too." How can our company progress with such a backward man as president? What can I possibly do?

A: Self-made men are sometimes not easy to convince, but don't give up hope. Try some of these approaches:

- Make your suggestions concrete. Propose your idea on paper, explaining why it would be an improvement over what exists now. Be sure to include figures.
- Try making your proposal periodically. I call this the mosquito approach. Some people have to be bitten many times before they catch on.
- Attempt to gain the support of a variety of people in your organization. Some people do not respond to the inherent logic of an idea. They need to know that many people support a proposal. Widespread approval convinces them.
- Try to get permission to do a project on a limited basis. This sometimes seems to be less threatening to those who fear change.
- Show your boss what your most direct competitors are doing. The success others have had with a similar approach is an excellent means of persuasion.
- Call in an expert to assess your proposal objectively.

Give your boss a little credit. He may not buy your idea right away, but on the other hand, if you were the president, would you immediately accept every idea presented to you?

Finally, keep those good ideas coming. The yes man who nods dutifully and doesn't come up with any good ideas will never amount to anything. Be careful not to become one of them simply because your proposals are not instantly greeted with enthusiasm.

"STOP SEXUAL ADVANCES."

Q: I am a woman manager at a large company, and men are always coming on to me and putting me in embarrassing situations. Even my subordinates sometimes act a bit fresh. I don't want to be tough because I will be thought of as being unfeminine. I'm told that I'm pretty. Maybe this makes my work situation worse. Can you offer any advice?

A: The situations you face are uncomfortable, but you must learn to control the manner in which men relate to you or your entire career will be in jeopardy.

Men often approach women in stages, testing to determine what women will accept and be receptive to. The problem you describe can begin with staring, move to sexual jokes, and from there to light touching and other inappropriately familiar behaviors.

You must stop the process at the very beginning. If you see signs of overfamiliarity, make it known in a clear, firm, yet nonangry manner that you find the action to be inappropriate and that you'd like the person to cease and desist forthwith.

When they comply with your request, thank them for their help in maintaining a high level of professionalism in your company. Don't be concerned about being thought of as unfeminine. You are not there as a woman; you are there as a capable professional.

Dress conservatively at all times. Keep your feminine spring dress at home. Keep yourself a bit removed in general, especially from after-dinner drinking. Alcohol will loosen their tongues, and the result may be unpleasant.

"EVENTUALLY, PEOPLE WILL GET EVEN."

Q: My view of managing people is, "Treat employees nicely and they'll treat you the same way." My boss, a longtime executive, insists that in business you've got to be an animal: "It's a dog-eat-dog world, and you've got to take whatever advantage you can whenever you can; otherwise you'll never make it." Who is correct?

A:

I want to talk about people like your boss. He is the guy who promises raises that he never gives, promises deliveries that never arrive on time, and promises performance that the product can never live up to.

This executive believes he's got the world fooled. He brags to his friends about his clever manipulations. There are, however, a few things this type of manager doesn't know.

He doesn't know that when he makes promises to his employees and doesn't keep his word, for some reason the machines keep getting stuck, the forklift is left out in the rain, whole files disappear never to be found again, his creative people sell their ideas to his competitor behind his back, and perfectly good parts get thrown out—accidentally, of course.

The point of all this is that you really can't mistreat people and get away with it, whether they are customers or employees. People will retaliate eventually.

We probably all know unethical executives like your boss. I wonder if they ever get more than 50 percent of their employees' potential. I also wonder who really winds up getting cheated.

Excellent managers believe they are like farmers and their real business is growing people. As a manager it's your job to get the most from your people. It is therefore your responsibility to help people grow, to nourish them, and to make sure they're protected from an overly strong sun. Your boss may be that overly strong sun. Follow your own instincts and you will reap a bountiful harvest.

"THEY DON'T
CALL IT STEALING."

Q: I simply can't get over some of our employees. They steal tools, staplers, scissors, and a whole assortment of products that our company makes. Last week I caught one of them walking out with a bag of one hundred Styrofoam coffee cups that he had obviously taken from the supply closet. When I stopped him and said, "What the hell do you think you're doing?" he looked at me as if I was crazy. He wanted to know why I was making such a big deal about a few lousy cups and intimated that I did my own stealing but that I was probably stealing other things. I insisted that he return the cups. This is a widespread problem. What do you suggest that we do?

A: Many managers are facing this kind of problem. Many more don't realize how pervasive this problem really is. The amount of company assets lost each year to employee theft is staggering. This immoral phenomenon is usually precipitated by one or a combination of reasons.

Sometimes employee morale is so low that employees use these tactics to get back at the company. In other situations, this thievery results from the notion that it's okay to take from the company since the company is rich and has thousands of these items; therefore, the company doesn't really need the object anyway. Still others believe that if they take the item, the company's insurance company will pay for it and, therefore, the company will not lose.

Some feel that employee theft is commonplace, everybody does it, employers understand and accept this, and the odd employee who doesn't do it is a sucker and a fool.

Finally, there is the employee who believes that the company owes him a debt since the company did not give the particular employee a raise, did not give him the bonus that was promised, or did not appropriately reward the employee for staying late, saving the company money, or doing the work of three employees.

Though I have described some of these bizarre philosophies, the truth is that no matter what rationale employees use to condone these practices, stealing is stealing, and as a crime, it must be met head-on.

It is my suggestion that you regard theft within the company in the same manner as you would a theft perpetrated by someone outside the company. If you allow someone, anyone, to steal from your company and do not respond in a strong and tough manner, you are merely inviting them to steal again. In this case, compassion will only create further abuse and, chances are, greater abuse.

In your particular company, where employee theft is commonplace, I would suggest that you post a code of ethical practice. In this code you should state that:

1. The company expects all of its employees to act with honesty and integrity in all of their dealings.
2. The taking or borrowing of company property is expressly forbidden (as examples list the items that most frequently disappear).
3. Employees who are discovered violating the code of ethical practice will be dismissed and face the possibility of criminal prosecution.

When conscience does not act as a deterrent to crime, the only recourse is punishment.

"THEY'RE CHEATING ON EXPENSES."

Q: I was on a business trip with three other managers from our company. The other managers decided to live it up and ordered an endless array of appetizers, lots of drinks, and the most lavish items on the menu. In addition, we were joined by three young ladies who giggled a lot, were not dressed like churchgoers, and ate and drank to great excess.

I should make clear that we were not with customers, prospects, or key suppliers. There was no business purpose to this very expensive experience. When the bill finally arrived, it came to a staggering amount. My face grew white. The other managers told me not to worry and that I should charge the bill to the company. They said I could explain to the company that we were romancing important customers and that if you want to make money, you have to spend money. I was stunned and said I couldn't do that. The other managers didn't understand me. They called me a do-gooder and wanted to know why I cared. After all, they explained, the company's paying for it.

Anyway, I couldn't bring myself to do this, so they just took the bill out of my hands and paid for it using the company credit card. They laughed at me and said that with my attitude I would never get anywhere in life.

I didn't say anything more about this to them that evening or since, but it has been bothering me. Am I a fuddy-duddy? Should I "get real" as they say? What do you think of this situation and what should I do?

A: I think that the actions of your peers constitutes theft—no more, no less. Your instincts were right. Don't worry about their insults. Your attitude is the correct one. Their attitudes are the ones that need fixing. Not only are your peers hurting the company, they are also hurting all the other people who are employed by the company. Here's how the phenomenon works:

Eventually, financially savvy executives in the company, whether they be the president, the chief financial officer, the controller, or a bookkeeper, will discover these excesses, and then everyone's travel, entertainment, or expense budget will become suspect. These dishonest practices will eventually create a companywide atmosphere of suspicion and hostility. Even innocent and honest employees will be grilled and interrogated. When this occurs, everyone suffers.

What should you as a concerned employee do when faced with this type of situation? In private, inform the offenders that you believe that their actions hurt the company and its employees and that, in your opinion, these practices are unethical.

Explain that if these dishonest behaviors continue, you will be forced to inform the appropriate people of their actions. If you believe your job could be threatened by this confrontation, then relay the information anonymously and in such a way that the information cannot be traced to you.

A company is like a delicate flower. It can't survive having petal after petal plucked from its stem.

Chapter Five

GETTING
AHEAD

Introduction

It may seem hard to believe, but in the daily melee of managerial life one's career often does not get the attention it rightfully deserves. Managers get caught up in the demands of work life and suddenly realize, "Hey, I'm not going anywhere." Often this awareness comes at raise-giving time or when someone else gets a promotion. Getting ahead must be a specific and well-thought-out goal. Good managers should be as interested in their own career progress as they are in helping their company to get ahead.

"What are the obstacles to my getting ahead?" must be the question. Managers, peers, or good friends will, if asked, answer this question honestly. Be careful not to dismiss their answers without carefully considering them. There may be truth to their words.

Many people believe they are getting ahead, but often this is nothing more than "wishin' and hopin'."

In order to get to the next level of his career, the manager requires additional skills and knowledge. Often the manager is afraid of getting more skills and knowledge, and afraid of failing. Many people live disappointing lives, their goals never having been realized. This chapter is for those people who don't plan for that to happen to them.

"WHY DO PROMOTIONS PASS ME BY?"

Q: I am thirty-three years old and I have been managing the same department for four years. I don't seem able to advance in my company. I am very ambitious but I seem to get passed up for promotions time and again. I'm getting very discouraged. Perhaps, something is lacking? Can you give me some suggestions?

A: Advancement in a company is not as difficult as it may seem because it is often based on your employer's perception of you. But let me give you some specific hints.

- Forget working nine to five: Employers like to surround themselves with dedicated people. Come in early and leave late. Don't worry, it *will* be noticed.
- Think of ways in which the company can save money and make more money. Anybody who can do this is perceived as valuable.
- Don't think in terms of *can't*; think in terms of *can*. Positive-thinking people forge ahead, while negative thinkers gain few friends and little respect.
- Work on your boss's priorities instead of your own. Don't assume that your boss is stupid and doesn't realize what is important. Chances are that he sees the larger picture while you are involved in a narrow piece.

Finally, be ready to change direction at a moment's notice without bemoaning previous efforts as wasted. Be ready to follow your boss's instincts wherever they may lead you. Your boss will only promote those individuals who are a willing part of the team.

"WHAT DO I NEED TO GET AHEAD?"

Q: I want to move up the management ladder to earn more money and have more prestige, and I am willing to work for my goals. How can I achieve them?

A: Your chances for career success can be greatly enhanced if you develop two critical skills:

The first is verbal skill. Make it your goal to be able to write an effective letter and present a detailed proposal in which you make yourself clearly understood.

When you interact with others, you demonstrate how well you can persuade, analyze, project, and solve problems. When you write a report, compose a speech, or dictate a memo, you prove your ability to take abstract thoughts, refine them, and present them in a lucid manner. If you want to improve your speech and composition, visit your bookstore or library. Select a useful text that includes exercises and projects to help develop thinking and writing skills. Also follow the proverb, "To study a subject one hundred times is good; to do so one hundred and one times is better."

The second skill you need is a facility with numbers. Don't become frightened; I'm merely referring to the basics of arithmetic and accounting. Understanding the relationship of numbers will help you understand finance, make projections, and interpret business information.

The higher you intend to climb as either a manager or an executive, the more you will need to develop these skills. Unfortunately, like many of us, you may be afraid of writing and afraid of numbers. Typically, these fears are carryovers from our school days.

One of the benefits of age, however, is that it brings maturity, stability, and discipline. These qualities can help you gain mastery over the areas I have described. You may even wish to consider private tutoring. The investment might well be the best one you'll ever make.

"I'M NOT THE SMARTEST GUY."

Q: I work hard and the department I manage produces quality work. Still I don't get promoted. I'm not the smartest guy in the world, but shouldn't I be rewarded for my superior performance?

A:

The answer to your problem lies in your own words. You say you're not the smartest guy in the world. Is this the message you give about yourself to the executive above you?

You may be unaware of the manner in which you present yourself to others. I often hear people making statements like, "I do the stupidest things sometimes." Their words may be an expression of lighthearted self-mockery, but other people may take these remarks seriously. After all, who is a better authority on you than you?

If you say you're not bright or that you make stupid mistakes, you must know what you are talking about. If you are prone to say, "I could never do that," people will believe you, and you'll never get the opportunity to find out whether you can or can't do the job.

If you say, "I never believed I would get this job," the people who gave it to you will wonder if they made a mistake. If you say, "I'm not fully awake till noon," don't expect to get a job that requires thinking at 9:00 A.M.

Each person, through his own descriptions of himself, projects a certain image to the world. Be careful with what you say about yourself. I guarantee that your negative descriptions will come back to haunt you.

"WHAT DO I HAVE, LEPROSY?"

Q: I can't figure it out. People with less experience and education are getting the promotions and I am still a middle manager. When I ask why, people look away and give me no answer. What do I have? Leprosy?

A: In today's society the outcast still exists, but for different reasons. In your case, lack of acceptance and the consequent lack of career advancement may be because of the clothes you wear, the way you comb or do not comb your hair, the cleanliness of your fingernails, the scuff marks on your shoes, or the jokes you tell.

Promotions are given to people who look and act the part. This can include their posture, the quality of their handshake, and their ability to maintain eye contact.

You should ask yourself some basic questions: What is your mood generally like? Are you usually upbeat and enthusiastic or often whining and melancholic? Are your gestures effective in making a point, or do you appear silly and awkward?

What is your vocal quality? Is your voice high-pitched and strained or is it resonant and confident-sounding? Do you clearly understand others? Can they understand you readily? What is the first impression you give to people? Do the people you work for find you interesting to talk to?

If your work performance is good, find out if your social skills are lacking. Your best method may be to ask your friends to level with you. If they're really your friends, they will. If you're smart, you'll listen.

"I AM
BURNING OUT."

Q: I feel exhausted all the time. I'm irritable, impatient, and, according to my peers, over-critical and burned out. I feel like throwing in the towel and running away to Alaska. I'm always under pressure. I feel I'm burning out like a match. Pretty soon, there'll be nothing left. What's going on?

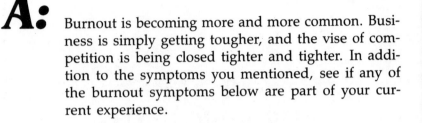

A: Burnout is becoming more and more common. Business is simply getting tougher, and the vise of competition is being closed tighter and tighter. In addition to the symptoms you mentioned, see if any of the burnout symptoms below are part of your current experience.

1. Are you less productive?
2. Are you sick more often?
3. Do you find it difficult to be creative?
4. Do you feel unappreciated?
5. Are you late for work?
6. Do you make more mistakes than before?
7. Do you avoid doing even trivial tasks?

If you have answered yes to a number of these questions, you may be suffering from burnout. It might be a good idea to consult a physician or at least take a small holiday if you can.

Burnout is caused by an excessive amount of stress, typically long-term or chronic stress. This is stress that doesn't go away, stress that is there to greet you every morning when you come to work, stress that's been there for weeks, months, sometimes years.

Persistent, excessive stress is a very dangerous thing. It's the stuff that causes nervous breakdowns and heart attacks. Chronic business stress comes from some situation in your work environment. It could be a negative change, person, or problem. This type of stress tends to improve if (1) in some way you fix the problem; (2) the problem goes away; or (3) you learn to react differently to the problem.

Temporary solutions that people have sought to relieve stress include myriad activities such as sports, television, gambling, or drinking alcohol. The tendency, however, is to overdo the solution and the solution then turns into an additional problem.

Don't be fooled by simplistic solutions. The symptoms of chronic stress do not just go away. Either the situation has to change or you have to change. And the sooner the better.

"ONE DAY WE'LL FIX THIS PROBLEM."

Q: I have a manager who works for me and does his daily job pretty well. The frustration I have with him is that when I bring up a problem, he nods and says, "Yep, one day we'll have to fix that." I know he'll never deal with the problem, and it irritates me. He's not going to get ahead with this attitude. Don't you agree?

A: Absolutely! Managers should be what I call problem eaters. They should pounce on problems they find and do their best to devour them.

Because problems in a business will impact directly or indirectly on the bottom line, they are important and need to be dealt with. I would not be happy with the Gary Cooper "yep" response you got either.

What I *do* like is the following scenario:

A manager at a meeting hears a problem. Briefly he jots it down because he doesn't want to forget it. Then, quietly and effectively, he solves it. His next action is to tell the person he reports to about the problem, and how he solved it.

This same manager is the guy who picks up the pieces of trash on the floor, jumps in to help when other people are out sick, and finds a way to solve the problem in shipping, even though it is not his responsibility. I like to watch this type of manager eventually become president.

The manager who doesn't even notice the problems around him is really an employee in a manager's position. The manager you described who does see a problem yet doesn't respond to it is himself a problem.

You may wish to use the following Problem-Solving Skills Checklist to assist you in your problem-solving skills.

Action Tool: Problem-Solving Skills Checklist

When attempting to solve a problem, ask yourself the following questions:

1. How did the problem occur?
2. Did something go wrong?
3. Were there unexpected results or outcomes?
4. Is something that once worked no longer working?

5. Is the problem people-centered?
6. Is the problem operational or functional?
7. Is the problem technical or mechanical?
8. Is the problem concrete or difficult to comprehend?
9. Is it an external or internal problem?
10. What effect is the problem having?
11. Is the problem common or uncommon?
12. What has previously been done in regard to this problem?
13. What have other companies done about this problem?
14. What knowledge might you need to acquire to solve this problem?
15. What do experts say about this problem? (Each field has its leaders who have written books, have given seminars, and are recognized as authorities on the subject.)
16. Who should be responsible for this problem?
17. Does this problem need to be solved? (Not all do.)
18. Do you list as many parts of the problem as you can?
19. What other problems have you faced that were similar to this problem?

"I HATE
OFFICE POLITICS."

 I'm a nice person. I manage my staff well and mind my own business. I don't get involved in office politics and being seen by the right people. My peers do this all the time. I don't see it as being important. Don't you agree that this kind of pandering is unnecessary?

A: It sounds as if you are one of those "nose to the grindstone" professionals who believe that success at work should be a reflection of accomplishments. After all, they told you in school that hard work is handsomely rewarded.

What they didn't tell you is that every human environment is a political one. This means that some people are interested in power, some people will attempt to enlist you as an ally, and some people will see you as competition to be eliminated. Some bosses will welcome your suggestions, while others will view you as an upstart who is trying to take over when you offer suggestions.

Internal public relations are an extremely important variable in your career. You can choose to play the part of purist and simply do your job, ignoring everything else. But be forewarned: You're taking a large risk. This is especially true when you are competent, because others may view you as a threat.

Sometimes the following scenario occurs:

1. The incompetent worker, sensing that he may not survive on the basis of his performance, develops political skills to protect his job.
2. The competent worker directs his efforts toward specific work achievements; he does not devote time to massaging egos and "being seen."
3. The incompetent worker climbs faster and not infrequently ends as supervisor of the competent one.

My point? Success at work depends on performance and public relations. Make sure you excel at both.

"I CAN'T MAKE A DECISION."

 Q: One of the toughest parts of my life as a manager is making decisions. I tend to get confused. I can usually make a good argument in either direction. The arguments seem to have equal validity. Because of this problem, I frequently put off important decisions. This causes significant difficulties for my employees, other department managers, and my boss, who goes crazy. Sometimes, he storms into my office and says, "Are you going to make the decision or not? If you don't, I will. Then you'll have to live with whatever decision I make." Is there anything I can do to improve in this area?

A: Don't be disheartened. Many people experience this problem. They simply camouflage it and blame their indecision on someone else. Use the following format in a step-by-step fashion and issues will become clearer for you.

1. Define what the issue is.
   a. What do you wish to decide? Why? Is it necessary? Why?
   b. What is the effect you wish to achieve from your decision? Write this down.
2. Delineate the possible options.
   a. Gather information to find additional options, using the following resources:
      (1) Books, magazine articles, and columns
      (2) Experts, consultants
      (3) Your past experiences
      (4) Other companies and organizations
      (5) Other managers and employees
      (6) Peers and friends
3. Think through each option.
   a. Write down each option.
   b. Consider all the positive and negative consequences of each option.
   c. Where possible, attach a weight to each consequence.
   d. Ask those who will be affected by the outcome of your decision to participate in the analysis.
4. Rethink your choices to see if you arrive at the same conclusion. Use the SOCS formula. Ask yourself these questions:
   a. Situation—what is my situation?
   b. Options—what are my options?
   c. Consequences—what are the consequences of each option?
   d. Simulation—find a way to test your solution by simulating it. Try it on a small experimental basis.
5. Design an implementation plan.

   a. Orient those who will be affected and win them over. They can make it succeed or fail.
   b. Plan a timetable for the implementation.
   c. Prepare all the necessary equipment and/ or services.
   d. Give yourself enough time. Don't rush into it.
6. Monitor and evaluate the decision.
   a. Monitor carefully and regularly to see if the desired results are occurring.
   b. Meet with managers, employees, customers, and vendors for feedback.
   c. Alterations may be necessary. Know this up front.

If you use these methods, those gray issues are gonna clear up, so put on a happy face.

"IT'S HERE
SOMEWHERE."

Q: I went to see a manager last week about an upcoming project. He was young and casually dressed, but what really unnerved me was his desk. It looked as if his file cabinet had fallen, and not having had the time to clean it up, he had piled all his papers on his desk. I figured that a man who was so disorganized could never be a good manager. I gave the assignment to someone else. What are your thoughts?

A: Many people react in a negative fashion to the disorderly office. They believe that the chaos they see is a reflection of an inability to organize, prioritize, and systematize work. They lose confidence in such individuals and aesthetically do not enjoy being in such a messy environment.

Apologies such as, "I've got to get this place cleaned up" don't alter the impression. They don't believe the owner of the messy desk when he says, "I know where everything is," especially if only minutes later he scratches his head to wonder, "Where did I put that thing?" It's not enough that he claims he can find everything. What will happen when he is out of the office and someone else has to find something?

I'm not saying, mind you, that people who keep disorderly desks are always inefficient and disorganized. The impression of the person, however, is not favorable.

When you meet people with this problem, you might remind them that a thorough cleanup can have four results:

1. They will find their work life easier.
2. People will think more highly of them.
3. They may get that long-sought promotion.
4. Their secretaries may stop buying voodoo dolls that bear an uncanny resemblance to their bosses.

"I'M TEMPTED TO LEAVE MY JOB."

Q: I have a very good-paying and important management position in my company. I have been offered more money by another company. I am not always happy with the way things are run where I am presently employed. Sometimes I think my current bosses are a bit crazy or at least dense. I am tempted to leave, but I have mixed feelings about it. What do you recommend?

A: Though the ancient saying, "If I am not for myself, then who will be for me?" is quite true, you need to be sure that a move will enhance your life and not diminish it.

Happiness in your prospective job does not depend only on money. It also depends on the type of work you will do. Will your new responsibilities be essentially the same or different? Will your work be challenging or will you be taking a step backward?

Your satisfaction will depend in large measure on the type of people with whom you work. Will they be resistant or cooperative? Will they welcome you aboard or will you be resented for replacing their buddy?

The type of company you will work for is also very important. Will you be treated well or will you resent its employee policies and procedures? Will you have good job security or will your employment be threatened by the job seeker who offers to perform your function for a few dollars less?

If your move involves a geographic change, you and your family will experience the healthy dose of stress that typically accompanies such relocations.

If you are experiencing craziness in your company, I'd like to remind you that you already know how to live with that craziness and cope with it. A new situation means starting all over again. Are the potential rewards really worth it?

Finally, you might try to analyze the reasons for your unhappiness with your current job. Are you unhappy with:

1. The type of work you are doing
2. The opportunities for advancement
3. Your relationship with your supervisor
4. Your relationship with your peers
5. Your relationship with your subordinates
6. Your compensation, benefits, or retirement plan

7. The company's culture
8. The company's progress

Is there spillover from your personal life? Are you possibly more unhappy with yourself than with your employer?

Review these issues, and you may discover that considering we live in an imperfect world, your present employment is a pretty good situation.

"SHOULD I THANK THE BOSS?"

 I recently got a promotion to division head and a nice raise. I felt it would be appropriate for me to write a note to my boss expressing my feelings. My peers disagreed and said he owed it to me. What do you think?

A: You are someone who is going to go far. Your instincts are right on target.

Too often managers are guilty of treating their bosses with the same negative attitude they accuse their bosses of having: They say, "He doesn't appreciate anything."

If your boss does something nice for you, of course you should thank him. Don't take the position that others take of "Hey, he's not doing me a favor; I worked for it!" This attitude will get you nowhere.

You may have worked for your raise, but your boss still chose to give it to you. It is a sign of his appreciation of your efforts, and the mark of a well-mannered person is to be appreciative. Such courtesy will gain you points.

Bosses, by the way, are vulnerable. They want to be appreciated and respected by their employees.

I wonder how many managers thank their bosses for being patient with them, answering their many questions, and understanding when they have to be absent for extended illness or because they are going through a family crisis.

I wonder how many managers tell their bosses that they think the boss did a good job on some project. Giving genuine compliments to a boss is part of a good boss-manager relationship.

My point? Remember that your boss is human: He bleeds when hurt and feels good when caressed with a warm word of genuine praise.

"I SHOULD HAVE BEEN PROMOTED."

 I can't tell you how angry I am. Last week, Linda, a manager who has been at our company for eight months, got a promotion over me. I've worked hard all year, volunteered for all kinds of projects that nobody wanted, saved the company big sums of money, and got them out of three big jams that were causing the company big problems—and this is my reward. Linda doesn't have my experience; she doesn't have my problem-solving ability; and she doesn't have my knowledge. And they promoted her over me. This is the last straw. I'm handing in my resignation. Don't you think I'm right? Wouldn't you do the same thing?

A: I can certainly understand your frustration, but I think you should stop and think for a moment.

If Linda is really not as valuable as you are, don't you think that it will become evident in the first month or two? When they give her assignments and she's not able to perform them or she can't do as well as you might, don't you think your superiors will see that? In other words, the ball game is not over yet. Linda may not be able to hold onto her job, and you'll be ready and capable of doing the job.

As a consultant, I've seen situations where a person gets passed up for a promotion only to discover that six weeks later he gets a promotion to an even bigger job than he had hoped for with greater responsibility and compensation.

Unfortunately, your superiors are only human and they will make mistakes in judgment. After all, in the course of our lives, you and I have made a few mistakes in judgment. It would be nice to say that our errors have always been small and insignificant, but you and I both know that this is not true. So temper your anger by remembering the fallibility of human beings.

Also remember that what happened to you is not forever. Actually, what happened to you is temporary. Life is not static. It is dynamic and ever changing. Chances are one year from now your situation will change, your company's situation will change, and with change comes opportunity.

As a salesperson (and if you're trying to get a promotion, believe me, you're selling yourself), you don't want to allow yourself to become paralyzed by rejection. A superior salesperson never takes *no* for an answer. He just tries to make the sale a different way.

My suggestion is that you accept what happened and fortify yourself to begin the battle again, this time with possibly a new tactic and a new target. Simply put, don't sink into bitterness, but rather strengthen yourself for the next bout in the ring.

Finally, if you speak to any successful older executive and ask him if he ever lost a promotion he dearly wanted, the response will probably be a smile and, "How much time do you have for me to answer that question?"

"I'M COMFORTABLE HERE."

Q: My friends can't understand me. I don't want another promotion. I don't want to leave this company. I like it here. I like my job for the most part. Sometimes, I do wish my job was a bit more interesting, but overall, I'm pretty happy. My boss thinks I'm doing a good job, but my friends shake their heads and say I'm crazy for not wanting a promotion. What should I do?

A: Let them continue to shake their heads. You stay right where you are. Unfortunately, we live in a society where the reigning philosophy dictates that we should all be scratching to get more and more and we should never be satisfied. The major problem with this type of thinking is that it promotes unhappiness on a forever basis, because you never have enough.

Hurray for you, and don't fall prey to the pressures around you. Ignore them. There's nothing wrong with being in one job for a long time, as long as you are doing a good job and feel fulfilled.

On the subject of being fulfilled, remember that no one in any job is fulfilled all of the time. If somebody tells you he loves his work 100 percent of the time, he is either lying or his head is in neutral gear.

There are, though, activities that you can do to make your work more appealing. Several of them are contained below:

- Vary your schedule. What you normally do in the A.M., do in the P.M. What was always done on Monday, do on Wednesday.
- Take on some new responsibilities and tasks that you would like to do but simply have not done before.
- Take a course. Read a book. Go to a seminar.
- Become more active with your trade organizations. Talk to the executive directors about what's going on in your industry. Do the same with the editors of your trade publications.
- Take it upon yourself to make some improvements in your department.
- Consider developing S.O.P.'s (standard operating policies) to assist others less experienced than you.
- Become a mentor to your most capable subordinate. Teach him how to improve.

- Put together a seminar or training program for your employees.
- Take an interest in the "numbers" part of your department—both financial and production dimensions. Contrast these with past years and the swings of seasonality.
- Take an interest in how other departments would like your department to function.

These suggestions can make your job more enjoyable. As to your friends, let them pursue the promotion treadmill for themselves. They are obviously unhappy people trying to become happy. You have already bypassed them on life's road. You are *already* happy.

EMPLOYER BILL OF RIGHTS

The purpose of this document is to provide perspective to employees in their treatment and view of employers.

Let it be known that every employer has these inalienable rights:

- To be treated with dignity and courtesy and without covert insults or sarcasm
- To be treated with honesty and integrity
- To expect that company resources will be treated with care and caution
- To receive quality work performance
- To expect that employees will maintain a high level of accuracy and that employees will learn from their mistakes
- To expect that employees will use their time carefully and wisely
- To expect that company privileges and benefits will not be abused
- To expect employees to ask questions if they do not know how to perform a task instead of leaving the task undone
- To expect employees to inform management if they cannot meet the agreed-upon schedule

To be informed when a person, machine, program, plan, or procedure is not working correctly

To expect that sincere and sustained efforts will be made to solve problems

To be informed if any employee is unhappy with his or her conditions of employment

To expect employees to act in a thinking and caring fashion about their function and the company as a whole

To expect that work will continue unabated when supervisors are not present

To expect that company policies and procedures will be followed

To expect the chain of command will be followed

To expect that employees will address issues of obvious waste and needless expense within their departments without being prompted to do so

To expect that employees will inform management when they perceive that their company is facing, or will face, a threat to its continued existence

To expect that employees will act as positive motivators of other employees

To expect that employees will present the company in a positive manner to customers, vendors, and others

EMPLOYEE
BILL OF RIGHTS

The purpose of this document is to provide perspective to employers in their treatment and view of employees.

Let it be known that every employee has these inalienable rights:

To be treated with dignity and courtesy and without insults or sarcasm

To receive equal treatment with other employees performing the same function in the company

To protest when provable prejudice or favoritism is practiced by a supervisor

To receive the necessary orientation and training that is required in order to perform the task satisfactorily

To be given the proper resources, material and human, and enough time to perform the task satisfactorily

To be given a reasonable amount of the supervisor's time within which pertinent questions can be asked and pressing problems can be solved

To receive constructive positive and negative feedback on work performance

To know the company's priorities for a particular function and to follow those priorities without incurring managerial dissatisfaction for doing so

To follow instructions from one supervisor that will not be contradicted by another supervisor

To receive fair and reasonable compensation commensurate with performance, level of responsibility, and market conditions

To receive truthful information about job security and opportunities for promotion

To be disciplined in private

To not have work performance discussed with another employee of similar rank and function

To present his side of a disagreement prior to conclusions being reached about the issue by management

To give input on company policies that directly affect him

To expect the company to be truthful and ethical in all dealings with him

To know by which criteria he will be evaluated

To make reasonable mistakes during the initial period of learning a new task

To expect the company to provide him with a work setting that will be conducive to the type of work being done

To be treated with as much respect as the employer, and without implication of inferiority or servitude

PROBLEM-SOLVING INDEX

This index will direct you to answers that will help you solve specific problems.